I believe that happiness should be taught to children of all ages. Relax Kids does just that!

Marneta Viegas makes an important contribution to the happiness and wellbeing of our next generation. Positivity is contagious and Relax Kids is infecting us all!

Dr David R Hamilton, Scientist, speaker and best-selling author of *Why Kindness is Good for You* and *How Your Mind Can Heal Your Body*

It's been wonderful to watch Marneta's work reach right around the world. If there is one thing that kids need but don't generally get these days, one thing that will stay with them and sustain them for the rest of their lives, it is the art and practice of relaxation. This is yet another fabulous collection of Marneta's meditations and visualizations which I am certain will revereberate right around the world. The wonderful thing is that as parents read the visualizations they also relax deeply with their children. Isn't that very clever?

Mike George, Author of *The Immune System of the Soul*

I'd recommend these books for any family that finds that life is just non-stop and wants a child-friendly way too wind down.

Antonia Chitty, Parenting and business author

The Magic Box is one of the few books that I use both at home with my children and at work with young people suffering from chronic physical health problems and pain. The multi-sensory visualisations give children and young people their own 'tool box' of relaxation skills to help them negotiate what is becoming an ever uncertain world. Marneta's books are invaluable at

i

helping to build our children's resilience.
Dr Fin Williams, Paediatric Clinical Psychologist

TESTIMONIALS

These meditations are a beautiful and easy route to helping your child relax and feel calm. They can be read to the child, or a child can help themselves directly. Adults will benefit too! I recommend Marneta Viegas's meditations to families across the globe.
Dr Julia Ronder, Consultant child and adolescent psychiatrist

My students love Relax Kids meditations. The beautifully crafted stories give them a few moments to stop, think, imagine and focus without condition or judgement.

Marneta uses a consistent and effective story formula that triggers visions and dreams which transcend cultures.

The wide variety of rich vocabulary used in these meditations linger in the children's minds long after class. One student said she started to believe she was 'extraordinary' the more she thought about the meaning of the word and how she could make sentences with it.
Natalie A Francis, Additional Learning Coordinator

I have had the absolute pleasure of seeing the effects that these super meditations have on school children as well adults with special needs. With both groups I saw instant relaxation and a lasting feeling of calm. A fabulous collection that will benefit anyone lucky enough to experience their power.
Kate West, Primary school teacher

This book helps you create that special family time that will capture precious childhood memories to treasure.
Gillian, Parent

RELAX KIDS
The Magic Box

52 Fantasy meditations
for Children (ages 5+)

RELAX KIDS
The Magic Box

52 Fantasy meditations
for Children (ages 5+)

Marneta Viegas

Illustrations by Nicola Wyldbore-Smith

OUR STREET
BOOKS

Winchester, UK
Washington, USA

JOHN HUNT PUBLISHING

First published by Our Street Books, 2014
Our Street Books is an imprint of John Hunt Publishing Ltd., 3 East St., Alresford,
Hampshire SO24 9EE, UK
office@jhpbooks.com
www.johnhuntpublishing.com
www.ourstreet-books.com

For distributor details and how to order please visit the 'Ordering' section on our website.

Design: Stuart Davies
Illustrations: Nicola Wyldbore-Smith

UK: Printed and bound by CPI Group (UK) Ltd, Croydon, CR0 4YY
US: Printed and bound by Thomson-Shore, 7300 West Joy Road, Dexter, MI 48130

We operate a distinctive and ethical publishing philosophy in all
areas of our business, from our global network of authors to
production and worldwide distribution.

CONTENTS

www.relaxkids.com

Thank you to my mother for introducing me to meditation when I was twelve, thank you to all my friends who have supported me along the way, thank you to all the Relax Kids coaches who have shared their ideas and suggestions.

Foreword

Social stories are a wonderful way for children to explore learning and mindfulness. Children love to tell stories, role-play stories and teach others what they learn from stories. Marneta has captured the creativity at the heart of childhood with imagery and stories to guide mindful meditation in children. Research supports that mindful meditation calms the brain, inspires creativity and enhances cognitive and social-emotional skills.

The Box of Magic is a gift of meditations children can do anytime, anywhere to get centered, experience peace and build a calmer inner life. With visual concepts such as the Magic Paint Brush, Superheroes and the Time Travel Machine, Marneta provides the words and actions needed to practice mindfulness as early as five years of age. The Box of Magic provides a beautiful and meaningful way for parents to connect with their children and for teachers to incorporate calming skills in the school day.

Marneta's Relax Kids creations build cognitive and social-emotional skills for all children but they have special meaning for children with anxiety, depression and anger as these children need actionable, accessible tools for self-regulation and mood management. Marneta has taken the guess-work out of helping your children develop calming skills with 52 meditations that are visually stunning and fun.

No other author is better suited to model for children, parents and teachers how to get calm and remain calm. As the author of over 20 books and relaxation CDs, Marneta is the princess of meditative calming for children. Her products are beautifully created, well-written and ready for immediate use, like a gift delivered to your door with a big red bow for learning and development.

Lynne Kenney, PsyD., Pediatric Psychologist, author, speaker
Author of *The Family Coach Method*

I

www.relaxkids.com

About the Author

Marneta Viegas set up Relax Kids in 2001. She had been running a successful children's entertainment business for thirteen years and noticed a change in children's behavior. Children seemed to be less able to sit still, listen and concentrate on her show. Using her degree in Performing Arts and techniques she had picked up from drama, singing and mime school combined with the meditation techniques she had learnt from a child, Marneta created a unique seven-step system for teaching children to relax. The classes were successful and Marneta now runs training for those who want to teach Relax Kids relaxation classes to children. Marneta has trained over a thousand people in her method from over 35 countries. Relax Kids is used in over half a million homes and schools worldwide.

If you would like more information about other Relax Kids products, relaxation classes and to train with Marneta, visit www.relaxkids.com

Marneta will be delighted to answer any emails
marneta@relaxkids.com

Relax Kids products

Books

Aladdin's Magic Carpet
52 meditations using fairy stories (ages 3+)
The Wishing Star
52 meditations for children (ages 5+)
The Pants of Peace
52 meditations for children (ages 6+)
How to be Happy
52 activities and games for children (ages 5+)
Be Brilliant
Positive activities and cards for children (ages 5+)

CDs

Princesses
Superheroes
Up up and away
Nature
Relax and De-stress
Believe and Achieve
Little Stars (under 5s)
Self-esteem
Concentration
Anger Management
Anxiety and Worry

Cards

Star Cards – a treasure box of 52 cards to help children see and
develop their inner qualities
Mood Cards – 52 cards for positive moods

Download a FREE relaxation pack
www.relaxkids.com/freepack

How to use this book

For parents and teachers

These reflections incorporate simple relaxation exercises and visualizations designed to improve children's self-esteem and confidence and reduce stress and anxiety.

Practiced regularly, these exercises can have a profound effect on children's mental, emotional and physical wellbeing.

Set the scene by playing some soft music. You may decide to pick a random page, or take a page each day or week, moving chronologically through the book.

The affirmation at the end of each meditation is intended for the adult to use as a means of focussing attention and creating an atmosphere conducive to the children's concentration. We recommend you read this first.

After a moment's silence together, read the words slowly, with pauses, allowing the child to use his or her imagination.

You may like to read the words and then let the child drift into sleep, or you may discuss what they experienced, asking them to describe what they saw and how they felt. You may let them compare what they saw in their minds to the pictures.

Parents can read meditations to children at the beginning of the day, after school, in the evening or at bedtime.

Teachers can fit Relax Kids into anytime of the school day. You don't need much room as children can listen to meditations sitting at their desk or crossed-legged on the floor. Try reading a meditation at registration, during assembly, at lunch time, during circle time, after physical education, before going home or before an exam.

If you are interested in introducing relaxation to your child, why not send them to a Relax Kids activity class? Classes incorporate dance and movement, games, stretches, peer massage, breathing, positive affirmations and visualisations.

Relax Kids also runs a training program if you are interested in teaching relaxation skills to children.

relax Kids

www.relaxkids.com

Magic Box

Close your eyes and be very still and take in a deep breath. Imagine there is a glittery box in front of you. This is a very special magic box, made of rainbow crystals. It is sparkling in the light. Spend a few moments watching the multi-colored crystals glimmer. The light is bouncing and dancing all over the room. It is a beautiful sight and makes you feel so happy inside. Take in a deep breath and then as you breathe out have a think about a question you would like to ask the magic box. It can be any question. Maybe you have something that is bothering or worrying you? Maybe you are not sure about something? Maybe you would like to know what to do next? Inside the magic box is an object which will give you a sign that will help answer your question. Each time you open the box, the object inside is different. The magic box always knows just what you need. Ask your question again and then stop and wait. Now open the box very slowly and put your hand inside. Touch the object. How does it feel? Is it smooth or jagged? Is it soft or hard? Is it warm or cold? How do you feel when you touch the object? Keep your hand on the object until you can work out what it is. The magic box is answering your question by showing you this object. At first you might not understand, but if you stay very still and think deeply, it will all make sense. Notice how you feel. Be aware of what is going on in your mind. Do you feel your question being answered? Stay very still and think about your question and the object and see if it makes sense. And now, when you are ready, thank the magic box for showing you an answer to your question and make a promise to come back when you have another question. Each time you have a question, come to your special magic box and let the box show you an answer with a different object.

Big Smile

Close your eyes and be very still. Think about something that makes you smile. Maybe it is a person or something you love doing or a place you love to visit. Now very gently feel yourself smiling. See if you can raise the corners of your mouth slightly and create a quiet inner smile. Feel your mouth gently curling and your lips softening. You feel relaxed and peaceful. Spend a few moments holding on to this lovely feeling you have created. Now focus your smile on your eyes. Keep your eyes closed and see if you can gently smile with your eyes. Feel your eyes becoming soft and gentle. Feel your eyes become 'smiling eyes'. Now, send this calming smile into your throat and down your neck. Feel your throat muscles relaxing. Start to appreciate your throat and voice and how amazing they are. Now see if you can smile in your heart. Let this sparkling smile travel to your heart. Feel your heart soften and fill up with love and joy. Feel your heart opening and feeling full of love and happiness as you smile inside. Imagine your heart is becoming so big. Let your heart open up and smile. You feel so happy and loving. Feel as if your heart is getting bigger and bigger and filling up with love and joy. Feel your heart filling up with kindness and compassion. Appreciate your heart for keeping you alive and circulating your blood. Now take this loving feeling into your lungs. Feel every fibre in your lungs relax as your lungs let go of all the sadness and grief. Feel your spongy lungs soaking up the love and smiles. Appreciate your lungs for bringing oxygen to your body. Now see if you can smile deep down in your tummy. Take your smile to your stomach and feel as if your whole stomach is relaxing and smiling. Now see if you can imagine that every cell in your body is smiling. If ever you feel tension or pain in a part of your body, you can try relaxing and smiling there and notice what happens. This smile is good to try when you feel anxious or angry.
Stay for as long as you wish, enjoying your big smile inside.

I remember to smile, I remember to smile.

Magic Paint Brush

Close your eyes, be very still and just relax. Imagine you are holding a paintbrush. This is a magic paintbrush and you can paint whatever you would like to have in your life. If you would like happiness in your life, you can paint lots of yellow and sunshine and people smiling. If you would like lots of love, you can paint pink and red with hearts and butterflies and people hugging and laughing. If you would like to be peaceful you can paint calming blues and greens and pictures of grass and clouds and people lying down relaxing. What picture would you like to paint today? Pick up the paintbrush and choose a color and let the brush move around the paper. Feel your mind being free as your arm moves. The paint brush is magic and as it moves, your arm follows. It is such a wonderful feeling. You just have to have a thought about what you would like in your life and the paintbrush paints it. If there are any worries, fears or sad thoughts, the paintbrush paints over them and fills the whole picture with only positive things. The more you see positive things, the happier you feel. You know that your life is in your hands and you can create whatever you would like. Enjoy creating your beautiful picture of positivity. As you paint your picture, repeat these positive words, 'I am creative. I am naturally creative. I allow creativity to flow through me. I use my hands to create. I use my body to create. I use my mind to create. Everything I do is unique and special. I take care to notice the beauty that is around me. I see the creativity and beauty in the nature that surrounds me. I see the vibrant colors and shapes and movement around me. I am discovering talents that I did not know that I had. I am unique and special. I am talented and gifted. I am creative. My thoughts are creative and I know how to use my thoughts to create a wonderful life. I am expressive. Everything I do is amazing. I am naturally creative.'
Enjoy creating your beautiful picture.

I am creative, I am creative.

Thank You

Close your eyes and be very still. Breathe in and out slowly. Take in a deep breath and breathe all the way out. Take in a deep breath and as you breathe out say thank you to your breath. It is keeping you alive and allowing you to have this wonderful life. Take in a deep breath and breathe out and say thank you to your amazing body. It is a wonderful machine. It works perfectly and lets you do so many things in your life. Say thank you to your legs for carrying you and letting you walk, run, skip, dance and play. Say thank you to your arms for letting you write, paint, create, hug and play games. Say thank you to your back for supporting you and keeping you upright and letting you bend and twist and stretch. Say thank you to your heart for pumping blood through your body and keeping you alive. Say thank you to all your other organs for doing their special job in their own clever way. Say thank you to your eyes for allowing you to see the wondrous things around you. Say thank you to your ears for letting you hear the sounds of the birds and music and every-thing around you. Say thank you to your nose that lets you smell delicious things but also the things you want to stay away from. Say thank you to your mouth for letting you taste so many different tastes. Say thank you to your brain for controlling your body and helping it work. Now think of all the things in your life that you are grateful for. Think about having a home to keep you warm and safe, having people in your life that love you. Think about how lucky you are to have good food. Spend some time saying thank you quietly in your mind. Now think about all your possessions and how lucky you are to have clean clothes and toys. Think about your favorite toy and feel so grateful and lucky. As you sit there quietly, feel very calm and appreciative. Feel a warm feeling of gratitude surround you like a blanket. Continue to breathe in and out gently as you feel grateful and happy. See how long you can keep this grateful feeling for.

I am grateful, I am grateful.

Relaxometer

Close your eyes and be very still. Breathe in and out slowly. Take in a deep breath and breathe all the way out. Breathe in slowly, and breathe out slowly. Just imagine you have a thermometer called a 'relaxometer' inside your body. The more stressed your thoughts are, the higher the relaxometer goes, into the red. The more calm and chilled you feel, the lower the thermometer goes until it is in the blue. You want to try and keep your relaxometer in the blue as much as possible. Take in a deep breath and breathe out. Breathe in, breathe out. Breathe in, breathe out. Focus on the relaxometer and imagine it slowly going down into the blue as you continue your breathing. Breathe in, breathe out, breathe in, breathe out, breathe in, breathe out, breathe in, breathe out. Watch as the relaxometer drops and you become cool and relaxed. Imagine you are standing under a shower of blue water. Feel the cooling blue river washing all over your body and washing away the stress. Feel the restful blue water, raining over and helping you feel relaxed and calm. Feel the blue water washing over your head and neck. Feel the cooling blue water washing over your back and chest. Notice the cooling water trickle over your arms and down your legs and feet. You feel calm and relaxed. You feel relaxed and peaceful. Breathe in, breathe out. Breathe in, breathe out. As you breathe in, imagine you are breathing in a cool blue light. As the blue light is entering your body, you feel cool and peaceful. Repeat to yourself, 'I am cool and peaceful. I am cool and peaceful. I am cool and peaceful.' Feel the blue light entering your chest and stomach and moving through your limbs. Feel the calming blue light moving through your head. You feel relaxed and calm. With each breath, you feel more and more relaxed. Breathe in, breathe out. Breathe in, breathe out. Breathe in, breathe out. Breathe in, breathe out. Now notice how calm and relaxed you feel. The relaxometer is all the way in the blue. You are totally relaxed and calm. You have done

this all by yourself. Look how easily you can relax and calm yourself down with your personal relaxometer. Remember that you can use this relaxometer any time when you need it.

Now, when you are ready, wiggle your fingers and toes, have a big stretch and open your eyes.

I calm and relaxed, I am calm and relaxed.

Special Message

Close your eyes and be very still. Breathe in and out slowly. Breathe in and out slowly. Someone who loves you very much has a personal message for you. It is a special message and it is just for you. Stay very quiet and still as you hear the secret message and notice how you feel as you listen to this amazing message. You are unique. You are unique. You are one of a kind. You are one of a kind. There is no one quite like you. There is no one quite like you. You are special. You are special. You are amazing. You are amazing. You are brilliant. You are brilliant. You are super. You are super. You are OK. You are OK. You are wonderful. You are wonderful. You are spectacular. You are spectacular. You are clever. You are clever. You are extraordinary. You are extraordinary. You are friendly. You are friendly. You are fun. You are fun. You are incredible. You are incredible. You are awesome. You are awesome. You are fabulous. You are fabulous. You are strong. You are strong. You are bright. You are bright. You are imaginative. You are imaginative. You are a star. You are a star. You are superb. You are superb. You are kind. You are kind. You are terrific. You are terrific. You are lovely. You are lovely. You are loved. You are loved. You are sweet. You are sweet. You are unique. You are unique. You are wonderful. You are wonderful. You are valuable. You are valuable. You are talented. You are talented. You are precious. You are precious. You are lucky. You are lucky. You are positive. You are positive. You are powerful. You are powerful. You are joyful. You are joyful. You are precious. You are precious. You are confident. You are confident. You are perfect just as you are. You are perfect just as you are. You are happy. You are happy. You are beautiful. You are beautiful. You are priceless. You are priceless. You are amazing. You are amazing. You are radiant. You are radiant. You are relaxed. You are relaxed. You are warm. You are warm. You are special. You are special. You are unique. You are unique. Spend a few moments, breathing in and out and think about how special and unique you are.

I am unique and special, I am unique and special.

Tropical Island

Close your eyes and be very still. Imagine you are on your own tropical island. Feel the warmth of the sun on your body as you sit on warm sand. Listen to the gentle sound of waves lapping against the shore. Look at the crystal turquoise-blue water. Spend a few moments watching the waves moving over the sand. Watch the rhythmic movement of the waves. Feel yourself becoming more calm and focussed as you breathe in and out. Enjoy the smell of salt air. Notice how you feel on this tranquil island. You feel so far away. It is a wonderful feeling. Spend some time enjoying being free from worry and tension. Feel the warm sun on your shoulders and feel the warm breeze on your face and hair. Feel the sand between your fingers and toes. Just relax and breathe. You feel calm and quiet and in control. As you sit there, you notice all the beauty around you. You notice the palm trees gently swaying in the breeze. You focus on the colorful birds and wildlife. You feel soft and quiet inside as you enjoy sitting on your own private tropical island. Feel the warmth of the sun on your body as you sit on warm sand. Listen to the gentle sound of waves lapping against the shore. Look at the crystal turquoise-blue water. Spend a few moments watching the waves moving over the sand. Watch the rhythmic movement of the waves. Feel your tension melting away as you watch the waves move over the sand. Notice how the sunlight sparkles on the water. Watch the sparkling water as it ripples gently. Smell the refreshing salt in the air. Feel yourself becoming more calm and focussed as you breathe in and out. As you sit make a list of all the things you are going to do to help you de-stress your life. Make a list of activities that you think will help you become calmer and more focussed. Make a list of three things you are going to promise to do to help you stay stress-free and happy. Spend a few moments on your tropical island in peace and quiet and making plans to keep this peace and quiet in your life. Keep focussing on what you need to

do to keep your life stress-free. Continue to enjoy breathing in and out slowly as you enjoy your own beautiful island.

I feel free, I feel free.

Mindfulness

Close your eyes and be very still. Breathe in and out slowly. Breathe in and blow all the way out slowly and steadily. Feel yourself becoming calm and relaxed. Take in a deep breath and breathe all the way out. As you stay there, feel your mind becoming still and quiet. Become aware of your body, starting with your feet. Concentrate just on your feet. Do your toes feel warm or cold? Notice the weight of your sock on your feet. Feel the texture of the fabric against your feet. How do your feet feel? Move up to the ankles, calves and knees. How does each part of your body feel? Become aware of your clothes as they touch each part of the body. Do you feel any tension in your legs? How light or heavy do your legs feel? Can you feel the backs of your legs against the chair or bed? Become aware of your thighs and then hips. Continue to breathe deeply and slowly. Now concentrate on your stomach. Feel your stomach moving as you breathe in and out. How does your stomach feel from the inside? Now notice your chest. Feel your lungs expanding as you breathe in and out. Now feel your heart. Can you feel your heart pumping? How does your heart feel? Now notice your back. How does it feel? Do you feel any tension in your back and shoulders? Take in a deep breath and let go and relax. Feel all the tightness in the shoulders melting away. Become aware of your arms and hands. Do they feel light or heavy? Focus on your neck and throat. How do they feel? Become aware of your eyes, your ears, your nose, your mouth and your chin. Take some time to notice each part of your face. How does it feel? Do you notice any tension? Concentrate on your scalp and your hair. Can you feel the hair on your head? Do you feel any tightness in your head? Focus on your head as you breathe in and out. Now notice how your whole body feels. Do you feel more relaxed?

I am aware of my body, I am aware of my body.

Energy Boost

Close your eyes and be very still. Breathe in and out slowly. Take in a deep breath and breathe all the way out. Breathe in slowly and breathe out slowly. Feel the softness of your breath going in and coming out again. Listen to the sound of your breathing. With each breath, feel yourself becoming more and more relaxed. Breathe in, breathe out. Breathe in, breathe out. Imagine you are under a shower of light. This is an energy shower. Thousands of tiny droplets of light and energy are raining over you. Feel the droplets dripping over your head and face. As soon as the droplets of light touch your head, you feel energized and revitalized. Every drop fills you with energy and makes you feel full of inspiration and motivation. Your brain is full of new ideas. Feel the drops of energy falling over your face and down your chin and neck. You feel so fresh as the light pours over your face. The shower of light continues and touches your shoulders and arms. Your arms feel full of energy. The shower of light is now pouring over your whole body including your legs and feet. Your legs feel energized and ready to launch into action. You feel so active and vibrant. Stand for a few more moments under this shower of energy and light and feel yourself becoming full of light and brightness. Breathe in light and breathe out light. Breathe in energy, breathe out energy. When you feel you are lacking energy and motivation in the future, imagine this shower of light and feel the drops of energy all over your body and watch how you start to feel energized and motivated. Think about all the things you could do with all this extra energy. Think about how great you would feel if you woke up every morning with all this extra energy. What would you do with this extra energy? Repeat to yourself in your mind, 'I feel full of energy and feel motivated. I feel full of energy and feel motivated. It feels good to be full of energy and feel motivated. I feel full of energy and feel motivated.'

I am energetic, I am energetic.

Garden

Close your eyes and be very still. Imagine you are sitting in a garden. The sun is shining, making the colors in the grass and flowers look bright and vibrant. You are surrounded by white daisies, yellow sunflowers, blue cornflowers and red poppies. The breeze is blowing gently and the flowers move delicately. It is almost as if they are dancing. Spend a few moments feeling relaxed and peaceful as you enjoy the sunshine and look at the colors. Feel the breeze on your face as you breathe in. As you are looking at the flowers, you notice the insects. Stay very quiet and see if you can hear the ants crawling over the grass and listen to the buzzing bees. Spend a few moments watching the ants and the bees and think about how they work together and co-operate. Just nearby, you see hundreds of ants carrying large loads. These tiny ants are working together to bring large pieces of food or shelter back to their colony. The ants are getting together in groups and balancing the load together. They know how to work in a team. Each insect has its own little task. On their own they would achieve very little, but as a team they do great things. The bees do the same. Each bee collects nectar from hundreds of flowers, takes it back to the hive and adds their little sample of nectar to the honeycomb. The bees work so well together. So many great things can be done by working together and cooperating. As you lie there in the peaceful garden, spend a few moments thinking about your life and how you work in a team. Do you like working on your own or do you prefer to work with others? Do you work well with others? Can you think of all the things you can do in a team? Make a list of all the activities that you need a group or a team for. Everything becomes much easier when you work in a team as long as each person does their job. Even chores and activities that don't seem that fun can be more fun when working in a team. Think about your friends and how much you enjoy working with them in teams. Think about how you enjoy playing in teams.

I am co-operative, I am co-operative.

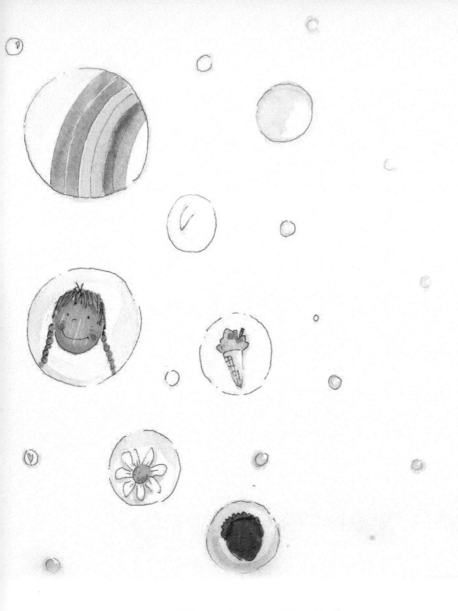

Happiness Switch

Close your eyes and be very still. Breathe in and out slowly. Breathe in and blow all the way out slowly and steadily. Think about something that makes you really, really happy. See if you can remember a happy memory. It might be playing with friends or being on holiday with your family. It might be sitting out in the sunshine or dancing or running. As you remember your happy memory, stay very still and imagine that you are there. Think about what you felt like and how happy you were and really remember how great the time was. Try and make everything in the memory really bright and exciting, make all the colors brighter and the noises louder. Make all the tastes stronger and the smells stronger too. See if you can really feel that you are there. What was it that made you feel happy? Try to imagine yourself back in that situation. Where are you? Who is with you? What are you wearing? What can you see? Try and remember as many details as you can. How were you feeling? Were you laughing or smiling? Try to remember how you felt in your stomach. How did you feel in your mind? Did you feel bubbles of happiness in your stomach? Did your heart tingle with happiness? Stay as still as possible and recall how you felt. Now, try to bring all these feelings back. Feel the tingling and bubbling sensations in your heart and stomach. Take in a deep breath and breathe in a feeling of happiness. And breathe out. Hold on to this happy feeling as you remember your special memory. Feel yourself smiling inside as you remember your happy memory. When your memory is very strong, gently squeeze your thumb and first finger together. Take in a deep breath, holding the memory as you squeeze your thumb and finger, and breathe out as slow as you can. Next time that you feel sad, all you have to do is close your eyes and put your thumb and first finger together again and you will remember your happy memory. This is your happiness switch. You can be anywhere in the world and take this with you and feel great.

I am happy, I am happy.

Secret Whispers

Close your eyes and be very still. Imagine you can hear a whisper in your ear. All the words are positive and make you feel wonderful. Listen to the positive whisper as you stay as still as you can. You are unique and individual. You have something special to offer. You are valuable and useful and special. Each person is valuable, useful and special in their own right and you are no less. You are special. No one can take this away from you. You are valuable, useful and special. Spend some time thinking about all the reasons why you are special. Think about your unique skills. The more you think positive and successful thoughts, the more you will achieve success. Everyday you become more and more successful. You believe in yourself. Your future is going to be amazing and you know that you will achieve success. You can achieve whatever you set out to achieve. You will be positive, stay focussed and concentrate on success. You know that your life is great and will get even better. You always feel motivated to do your best. You do the best that you can do. Success is doing the best you can do. You are motivated to work hard and achieve and do the best that you can do. Success is not just to do with money and fame. Success is to do with hard work, positive focus and strength of character. You use your thoughts to focus on your life and your work and your skills and talents. You commit to having only positive thoughts about your work, your skills and your life. You stay positive. You think about your future and look forward to a positive future where you do well. You stay positive. You know that you will be successful in the future and start to work hard to achieve that success. You are authentic and everything you do is with honesty and respect. You have all the skills and talents needed to achieve success. You are successful and you will be successful in everything you do. You feel confident about yourself and feel motivated to achieve success. You know your future will be great. You have all the intelligence and skills that you need to be successful. Spend a few moments thinking about those skills and thinking how you can increase them.

Each day I achieve success in everything I do.

Wonderful You

Close your eyes and be very still. Become aware of your eyes. See if you can relax the muscles at the backs of the eyes. Feel your eyes becoming soft and relaxed. Spend a few moments thinking about your eyes and how incredible they are. They allow you to see everything that is going on in your world. Become aware of your ears. Spend a few moments listening to the sounds in the room. Appreciate the wonder of your ears. They allow you to hear everything in your world. Become aware of your mouth, your tongue and your voice. Spend a few moments appreciating

them and being grateful for your voice that allows you to express your needs and feelings. Become aware of your chest and lungs. Feel your chest rising as you breathe in and falling as you breathe out. Each breath is sending oxygen into your body and keeping you alive. Spend a few moments appreciating the wonder of your breathing. Become aware of your heart. Can you feel it beating? Your heart constantly pumps around your body, keeping you alive. Spend some time thinking how amazing your heart is, as it continues to beat. Become aware of your stomach and digestive system. Think about how it turns your food into fuel that keeps your body alive. Spend a few moments appreciating your stomach. Become aware of your limbs. Spend some time appreciating your legs and arms and thinking about how they help you walk, run, work and play. Now, think about your whole body and how magnificent it is. Appreciate every part of your body. Even if there are parts of your body that don't always work exactly how you would like them to, or don't look exactly how you would like, remind yourself that your body is an amazing instrument. It works like clockwork and is an incredible machine. You can use your body for anything you want to do. You can express all your feelings through your body. When you are happy, you can sing, dance, laugh and smile. When you are sad, you might cry tears. When you are angry, you might shout and stamp. When you are embarrassed, you may blush. When you are nervous, you might shake. Whatever you are feeling inside, your body expresses it on the outside. Your body is amazing. You are amazing.

I am amazing, I am amazing

33

Just Relax

Close your eyes and be very still. Spend a few moments relaxing the parts of your body that you usually hold tension in. Relax your shoulders, relax your neck, relax your jaw and throat. Let everything around you fade into the background as you concentrate on your body. Spend some time letting thoughts of the past and the future go as you stay present and aware. Stay focussed and aware in the now, the present moment, this moment. Take in a deep breath and breathe out slowly and gently. Notice how the air moves in and out of your body. You are now going to take a tour of your body, noticing any tension. Start at your feet. Concentrate only on your feet. Do your toes feel warm or cold? Continue to breathe in and out deeply as you concentrate on your feet. How light or heavy do they feel? Move up to the ankles, calves and knees. How does each part of your body feel? Become aware of your clothes as they touch each part of the body. Do you feel any tension in your legs? Become aware of your thighs and then hips. Feel your buttocks and hips against the chair. What sensations do you feel in your legs and hips? Continue to breathe deeply. Concentrate on your stomach. Feel your stomach moving as you breathe in and out. How does your stomach feel from the inside? Become aware of your stomach and digestive system. Just observe what is happening. Bring your awareness up to the chest. Feel your lungs expanding as you breathe in and out. Bring your attention to your heart. Feel your heart pumping. Spend sometime being aware of your internal organs. Become aware of your spine and how it is relaxed into the chair. How does your spine feel? Do you feel any tension in your spine? Become aware of your shoulders. Do you feel any tightness in your shoulders? Concentrate on your shoulders and let go of any tightness. Become aware of your arms and hands. Do they feel light or heavy? Concentrate on your neck and throat. Become aware of your neck and throat. Become aware of your eyes, your ears, your nose, your mouth and your chin. Take some time to notice each part of your face. How does it feel? Do you notice any tension? Now, let everything go and just relax.

I am relaxed, I am relaxed.

Time Travel Machine

Close your eyes and be very still. Imagine in front of you is the most incredible Time Travel Machine. Walk all around the machine and notice how you start to feel excited as you realize this machine can take you all the way into the past. This machine is amazing. Find the door and step inside. Take some time to listen to all the sounds around you. It is very quiet here. All the

sounds from outside are shut out and you can only hear the low hum of the machine in standby and the sound of your breathing. Breathe in, breathe out. Breathe in, breathe out. Take a moment to enjoy the quiet. Sit down and put on your seat belt. It is time to start the machine. Can you see the big red lever right above your head? Pull it down. In front of you are lots of multi-coloured buttons and switches. There are pictures and numbers on each button. On each picture is a time in history. You see the Stone Age, Egyptians, Romans, Vikings, Medieval times, Tudors, Elizabethans and Victorians. Can you see any others? Look at the pictures and choose which time you would like to go to. If you know the exact time, you can punch in the date and the machine will take you to that exact date and time. Now hold tight onto your seat as the time machine whizzes and whirs into action. You can feel your whole body moving as you are catapulted backwards through time. It is an invigorating feeling. You feel totally safe and secure in the huge machine. You don't need to worry about anything. The machine comes to a gentle stand still. Look through the front window and you find yourself back in time. Where are you? How do you feel? Undo your seat belt and step out of the machine. Walk around and be free to go on your own adventure. Feel free to explore this wonderful time and maybe learn things you might not have known before about this time in history.

And now, when you are ready, step back into the machine, sit down and put on your seatbelt. Punch in the year that will take you back to your life and your world as you know it. Spend a few moments, thinking about where you have been and how different life was then to how life is now.

I am imaginative, I am imaginative.

Superheroes

Close your eyes and be very still. Imagine that in front of you is a superhero cloak. This is a magical cloak that is invisible to everyone else. When you put it on, you have special superhero powers. These powers help you in your life. Look at the cloak. It seems to be made of tiny particles of light. It is almost see-through. It is glimmering as the tiny particles of light twinkle. Touch the cloak and you can feel its power. As your hand touches the cloak, you feel a gentle current of power shudder through your whole body. It is a lovely feeling. It feels wonderful. This cloak can give you any super power that you need. What do you need today? Do you need to feel peaceful and quiet? Do you need the peace power? Do you need to feel happy and bright? Do you need the happiness power? Do you need to feel brave and strong? Do you need the strength power? Do you need to feel confident? Do you need the confidence power? What do you need today? Peace? Love? Happiness? Strength? Confidence? When you have chosen the power you need for today, take the cloak and put it on. Remember that this cloak is invisible to everyone else. As soon as it touches your shoulders and back, you feel a surge of energy and power come from deep inside you. The cloak is helping you find your inner power. You have this power inside you and the cloak helps you to feel it strongly. Can you feel this amazing power? Can you feel your amazing power? What does it feel like? Where can you feel it? Is the power in your stomach or chest or head? Where is it? Take in a deep breath and breathe in this power. As you breathe out, feel the power coming from your mouth. Breathe in, breathe out, breathe in, breathe out, breathe in, breathe out. Feel yourself smiling inside knowing that you are so strong and full of this amazing power. If anyone says anything negative or tries to hurt your feelings or does something unkind, you know you will be OK because the cloak is protecting you. Your powers are protecting you. All unkind words will bounce off your superhero cloak. Spend a few moments, feeling powerful, like a superhero.

I am powerful,
I am powerful.

Video Game

Close your eyes and be very still. Imagine you are in your own video game. This is an adventure game where you can go to all sorts of exciting places. On your adventure, you have to catch falling stars and search for stars in hidden places. The more stars you collect, the higher your score will be. These are special stars. They will help you feel confident. The more stars you collect, the more confident you feel inside. But, you have to watch out for the blobs! These are little creatures who want to take your self-confidence away and make you feel weak and unhappy. These are your enemies. They make you weak. They don't like to see you smiling and happy. So, watch out for the blobs. Whenever you see a blob, duck down or jump up high and float in the sky to avoid them. Are you ready for your adventure? You find yourself in a strange and colorful land. Everything is topsy turvy. Purple trees appear to be floating in the air. Clouds seem to be bouncing along

in the ground. Blue grass is growing and animals are walking up the sides of houses. It is a wonderful magical land. Take time to appreciate this new place as you look for the stars. Can you see any stars? When you see one, just touch it with your finger and it will pop and disappear as it adds to your confidence score. Have you seen any blobs? If a blob touches you, you lose a point and your score goes down. Try to dodge as many blobs as possible. It is the next level now and you find yourself in the mountains, you have to climb mountains and search in caves looking for the stars. What can you see? Have you found any stars? How do you feel? Next you find yourself in a desert. The stars are hidden in the sand and you have to uncover them. The blobs can catch you easily as there is nowhere to hide. Have you collected lots of stars? How do you feel? The next part of the game is in a frozen city. Everything is blue and cold. You have to keep moving to keep warm as you collect the stars and increase your confidence. How many stars have you found? How do you feel? The final level is your choice. You can go to the magical garden or dinosaur island or the fairy dell. Where would you like to go? How many stars have you found? How do you feel? And now, you have collected so many confidence stars. You notice how confident you feel. You feel full of self-confidence and feel yourself growing taller and taller. Spend a moment enjoying feeling full of confidence.

I am confident, I am confident.

Brain Food

Close your eyes and be very still. Breathe in and out slowly. Breathe in and breathe all the way out slowly and steadily. You are now going to have some brain food. Brain food is a special relaxing thought that helps calm your brain and mind down. It will give your brain a chance to relax and revitalize you. As you stay there very calm, continue to breathe in and out and let these words wash all over your mind and brain: I am calm, I am quiet. I feel relaxed and peaceful. I am calm, I am quiet. I feel relaxed and peaceful. I stay calm, I stay quiet. I breathe in calm, I breathe out peace. I feel a sense of calm in my body. I allow my body to relax and become peaceful. I allow my thoughts to become calm and peaceful. I feel in control. I breathe in and out slowly and steadily. I feel calm and balanced. I feel a sense of calm and tranquility all around me. I feel cool and quiet. I allow the tension in my body to slowly melt away. I feel relaxed and free of tension. I feel relaxed and quiet. My head is cool. My shoulders are relaxed. I allow all the tension in my shoulders to melt away. I feel calm and relaxed. My chest is relaxed. I feel calm and relaxed. My stomach is free of tension. I allow all the tightness around my shoulders to relax. My legs are relaxed. I allow the muscles in my legs to relax. I feel totally calm and relaxed. I let go completely and relax. I take in a deep breath and breathe out slowly and gently. I am calm, I am calm, I am calm. I let all anxiety and tension float away. As I breathe in and out, I let go of all tension in my body and mind. I allow all worrying and upsetting thoughts to drift away. I stay focussed on staying calm and relaxed. I enjoy the feeling of being relaxed. I enjoy being calm and quiet.

I am calm, I am calm.

tension

anxiety

relax

quiet

calm

43

Worry Tree

Close your eyes and be very still. Breathe in and out slowly. Breathe in and breathe all the way out slowly and steadily. Feel the softness of your breath going in and coming out again. Listen to the sound of your breathing. With each breath, feel yourself becoming more and more relaxed. Breathe in, breathe out. Breathe in, breathe out. Now, become aware of your shoulders. How do your shoulders feel? Are they tense and feel as if they are near your ears or are they soft and relaxed? How do they feel? Are they tense or relaxed? Have a think about what could be making your shoulders tense? Are you worried about something? Are you feeling stressed? Are you tense? For a few moments, see if you can let your worries disappear and just relax. See if you can let your shoulders go and feel all the muscles around your neck and shoulders relaxing. Now become aware of your stomach. How does it feel? Is it tense and knotted or soft and relaxed? Have a think about what could be making your stomach so tense? Are you feeling nervous or anxious about something? For a few moments let your nervous feelings go and see if you can relax your stomach. Relax. Relax. Relax and let go completely. Imagine for a moment that you can see all your worries in front of you. See them in as much detail as possible. If you can't see them, just get a sense or a feeling of them. How do your worries make you feel? Now, imagine there is a beautiful worry tree. You can write your worries on pieces of paper and hang them on the worry tree. Once you have put the worries on the worry tree, the worries are no longer your problem. The worry tree will take care of them. You feel as if your worries are slowly fading away. See your worries becoming smaller and smaller, and smaller. Take in a deep breath through your nose and breathe out slowly. As you breathe out, feel all your worries blowing away. Feel yourself becoming soft and relaxed. Your worries are now so small that they are hardly visible. How do

you feel now? Whenever you have any worries, you can just put them on the worry tree.

I am free, I am free.

Rainbow

Close your eyes and be very still. Imagine you have a rainbow inside your body. Your body is full of all the colors of the rainbow. The rainbow starts at your feet. Imagine your feet and legs are filled with rainbow-red light. It is strong and vibrant.

Feel your legs are full of red light. Breathe in red light and send it all the way to your legs and feet. This red light makes you feel strong and stable. Keep this rainbow-red light in your legs and feet. Now imagine your tummy area is full of bright orange light. It is strong and vibrant. Feel this bright light in your tummy. Breathe in orange light and send it all the way down to your tummy. The orange light makes you feel full of energy. It makes you feel joyful and creative. Now imagine your waist area is full of bright yellow light. It is balanced and powerful. Feel this bright light around your waist. Breathe in yellow light and send it all the way down to your waist. The yellow light makes you feel full of power. It makes you feel balanced and confident. Now imagine your chest area is full of bright green light. It is loving and kind. Feel this bright light in your chest. Breathe in green light and let it fill your chest area. The green light makes you feel full of love. It makes you feel loving and kind. Now imagine your neck is full of bright blue light. It is peaceful and calm. Feel this bright light in your neck and mouth area. Breathe in blue light and feel it going to your neck. The blue light makes you feel full of calm. It makes you feel peaceful. Now imagine your forehead is full of indigo light. It feels so strong. Feel this bright light in your forehead. Breathe in indigo light and send it all the way up to your forehead. The indigo light helps you concentrate and focus. It makes you feel still and focussed. Now imagine the very top of your head is full of violet light. It is so bright and strong. Feel this bright light in the top of your head. Breathe in violet light and send it all the way up to the top of your head The violet light makes you feel full of energy and creativity. It makes you feel creative and imaginative. It makes you feel content. Spend a few moments staying still and thinking about and feeling this amazing rainbow in your body. You can use these rainbow colors whenever you need them.

I am bright, I am bright.

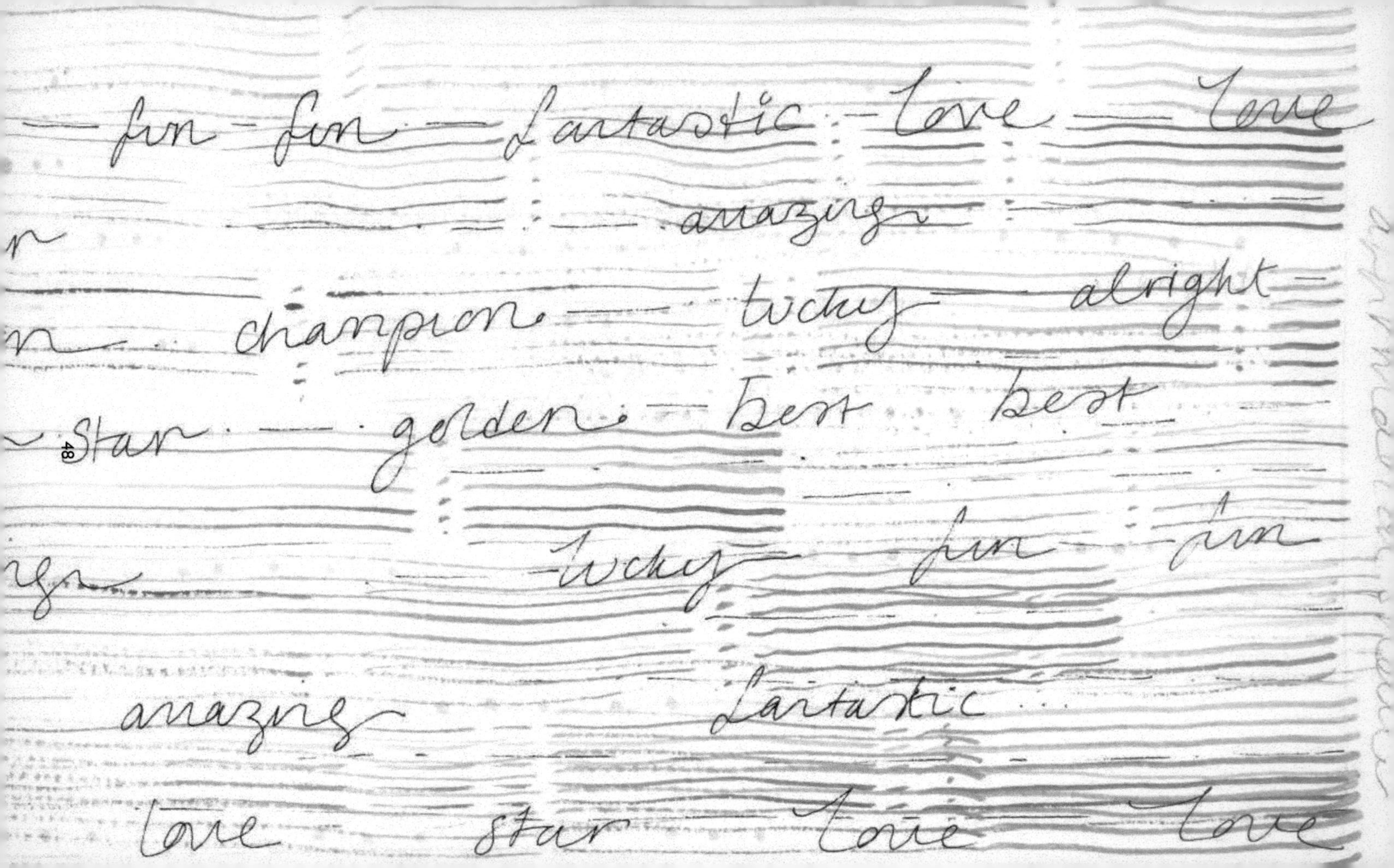

fun — fun — fantastic — love — love

amazing

champion — tricky — alright

star — golden — beer — best

tricky — fun — fun

tricky

amazing

fantastic

love — star — love — love

Affirmation Shower

Close your eyes and be very still. Breathe in and out slowly. Breathe in and breathe all the way out slowly and steadily. You are going to take an affirmation shower. An affirmation is something positive you say to yourself to help you feel great. Imagine you are standing under a wonderful shower of light. Stay very still and imagine that this shower is washing over every part of your body. Imagine that this is a healing shower and whenever it touches you, you feel more and more relaxed. Feel as if positive words are reaching inside every organ, every muscle and every cell. Feel as if the positive words are washing over you. Each time you breathe in, feel as if you are breathing in positive words. Stand under the shower and listen to the positive words. Feel the positive words touching your mind and body as the shower washes over you. You are amazing, you are amazing, you are great, you are great, you are big-hearted, you are big-hearted, you are super, you are super, you are beautiful, you are beautiful, you are positive, you are positive, you are good, you are good, you are a champion, you are a champion, you are alright, you are alright, you are OK, you are OK, you are special, you are special, you are fantastic, you are fantastic, you are incredible, you are incredible, you are wonderful, you are wonderful, you are fabulous, you are fabulous, you are brave, you are brave, you are bright, you are bright, you are smart, you are smart, you are cool, you are cool, you are brilliant, you are brilliant, you are powerful, you are powerful, you are positive, you are positive. you are unique and special, you are unique and special.

And now ask yourself, how do you feel? Continue to enjoy feeling energized from this affirmation shower. Now, when you are ready, wiggle your fingers and toes, have a big stretch and open your eyes.

I am amazing, I am amazing.

Dream Factory

Close your eyes and be very still. Imagine you are in a dream factory. This is a special place to think about what you would like to have in your future. It is the place to dream your dreams and create goals.

Spend a few moments thinking about yourself and what makes you special. What are you good at? What are your favorite activities? What do you love doing? Do you love sport? Do you love being on land or on water? Do you love art and crafts? Do you love cooking? Do you love being in nature? Do you love dancing? Do you love making things? Do you love reading? Do you love traveling? Do you love exploring? Do you love looking after people? Do you like playing music? Do you love investigating things? Do you love animals? Do you love gardening? Do you like acting? Do you love history? Do you love finding out how things work? Do you love being with people? Have a think about all the things that you are good at and see if you can identify your own personal talents and greatness. If you could do whatever you wanted to in the world what would it be? If no one was stopping you, what would you love to do? If you could go wherever you wanted, where would it be? Spend sometime visualizing whatever it is you would love to do. Enjoy each detail and imagine that you are there. See the picture in as much detail as possible. Now, imagine that there is a piece of paper and a pen in front of you and you are writing down your goals. Write down all the things you would like to achieve in your life. When you have finished, take the piece of paper and fold it up and put it in a very special place inside the dream factory. If in the future you would like to add to your list of dreams and goals, you can just come back to the paper and write down your new goals. It doesn't matter how high your aims and goals are, if you are determined and focussed and really, really want them, you can do anything! When you have hidden the paper in the dream factory, take in a deep breath and say to yourself, 'I can do whatever I want to do. I can do whatever I want to do.' Now, in your mind make a plan to do something small that takes you one step closer to your goal. It may be that you take up a new hobby or practice something a little more. Even if it is only a little step, it doesn't matter as it is one little step towards your goal and if you do this everyday, you can achieve whatever you want.

I am free to dream, I am free to dream.

Radio

Close your eyes and be very still. Spend a few moments watching your breathing. Listen to the sound of your breathing. With each breath, feel yourself becoming more and more relaxed. Breathe in, breathe out. Breathe in, breathe out. Imagine in front of you is a radio. This radio makes you feel happy as soon as you switch it on because it only broadcasts positive sounds and words. The radio tells you how amazing and wonderful you are. Are you ready to listen? You are wonderful. You have a fit and healthy body that allows you to work hard and play. Think about how amazing your body is. Think about how your eyes, ears, mouth and nose work to help you experience everything around you. Your body is a strong and powerful machine that works perfectly to allow you to live your life to the full. As you breathe in, appreciate and thank your body for doing its job and allowing you to eat, work, dance and play. You have a powerful mind that allows you to think and come up with new ideas. Spend a few moments thinking about your brain and your mind and thinking about how lucky you are to have such an amazing brain. You also have so many positive qualities that make you special. Spend some time thinking about your personality and your qualities and all the things that make you special. Which of these qualities do you have? You are strong, brave and courageous. You are clever bright and intelligent. You are fun, funny and lively. You are happy cheerful and joyful. You are kind thoughtful and caring. You are generous, giving and open-hearted. You are creative, imaginative and artistic. You are powerful, great and brilliant. You are individual, unique and special. You are appreciative, positive and inspiring. You are incredible, magnificent and amazing. You are so great and you have so many good qualities and things that make you amazing. Spend some time thinking about why it is good to be you. No matter what anyone says, you know that you are amazing and have an amazing body, mind,

and brain and so many special qualities that make you unique and perfect.

I am OK just the way I am, I am OK just the way I am.

Treasure Dragon

Close your eyes and be very still. Imagine you are on a magical, mystical island. This is Dragon Island. You look around and see that you are surrounded by trees. It is very wet and swampy and you see ferns growing in the undergrowth. Everywhere is very green and lush. Listen to the sounds of your footsteps as you slosh through the mud. Notice the damp smell of the swamp. As you walk on, you come to some rocks. You notice an opening and walk towards a cave. This is a dragon cave. You don't need to be afraid as this is your own special dragon. He looks after you and protects you from harm. Step into the cave. Stand still for a moment and notice how silent it is. Stay as still as you can. If you stay very still your dragon will come out to greet you. The dragon steps out slowly from the darkness. You are great friends and you go up to your dragon and hug him. Feel his smooth scales. Now your dragon has a special job to do. He guards your personal treasures. He is your own treasure dragon. He guards the most important things in the world. He guards your inner peace and calm, your love, your happiness and joy. Whenever the monsters of worry, anger, stress and fear creep up, they come to try and take away your treasures. Your friendly dragon looks after these treasures. As soon as he sees a monster approaching, he breathes his magic fire on the monsters and they shrivel up and disappear. Whenever you notice a monster of worry or anger or upset coming, you just have to call for your dragon and ask him to send them away. Watch as he breathes his breath of fire on the monsters, making them shrivel and disappear. You can join in with your dragon and breathe the monsters away. Stay very still and take a deep breath in and breathe out slowly. As you breathe out slowly, imagine you are breathing fire like a dragon and making the monsters disappear. You see how your dragon is protecting your valuable treasures of peace, love and joy. He knows that you will need them throughout your life and so keeps them safe for when you need them. Say thank you to your dragon and promise to visit him again. Remember to call him when the monsters of anxiety, anger and sadness visit you.

I am full of treasure, I am full of treasure.

Magic Castle

Close your eyes and be very still. Imagine you are in a magical land where anything can happen. All your questions can be answered, worries are taken away and dreams come true in this special place. It is a very special place and you can come here whenever you wish. Follow the winding pathway to your magic castle. You notice a huge door. What color is the door? The door is locked, but inside your pocket you have a key. Only you can open this castle door with your own personal key. Turn the key in the lock and hear the door creak open slowly. Step inside and listen to the quiet. It is quite dark inside the castle but you notice floating candles are lighting your way. The candles look as though they are dancing in the air. The flickering candles lead you up a stone staircase and through a huge corridor. You stop at a golden door. It has a question mark on it. Inside is the room of answers. Before you go in, have a think about what question you would like answered. Do you have a problem that you need help with? Maybe you are not sure what to do about a certain situation? What question would you like to ask? Spend a few moments thinking about your question. And now when you are ready, turn the handle and open the golden door. You look around and you notice a huge comfortable chair. Go up to the chair. What color is it? Sit down and notice how soft it feels to touch and how comfortable it is. Take some time to enjoy being in this special chair. And now, ask your question. Repeat the question slowly three times. Stay very still and calm. You notice a screen in front of you. As you sit there in the silence, you see images and words start to appear on the screen. These words and images are the answers to your question. The screen shows you exactly what you need to see. Look carefully. What words and images do you see appearing? Allow the images to become brighter and brighter. See your question being answered clearly. Spend a few moments thinking about the answer. And now when you are ready and your question is answered, get out of the chair, open the door and step down the candlelit staircase and out of the huge castle door and back down the pathway.

I have all the answers inside, I have all the answers inside.

giving
creative
powerful
magnificent
quiet
generous
great
artistic
peaceful
special
amazing

Positive Phone

Close your eyes and be very still. Breathe in and out slowly. Breathe in and breathe all the way out slowly and steadily. Imagine you are on the telephone. This is a special telephone that only tells you wonderful things about yourself. After you have listened to this telephone for a while, you feel special inside. After listening to the positive words, you feel full of positivity. After listening to the talking telephone, you are able to believe in yourself and believe that you are special and amazing. No matter what other people say, you only believe in the positive things and don't listen to anything negative. Put the handset to your ear and listen to the voice coming out of the phone. You are strong, you are strong, you are strong. You are brave, you are brave, you are brave. You are joyful, you are joyful, you are joyful. You are kind, you are kind, you are kind. You are thoughtful, you are thoughtful, you are thoughtful. You are caring, you are caring, you are caring. You are generous, you are generous, you are generous. You are giving, you are giving, you are giving. You are open-hearted, you are open-hearted, you are open-hearted. You are creative, you are creative, you are creative. You are imaginative, you are imaginative, you are imaginative. You are artistic, you are artistic, you are artistic. You are powerful, you are powerful, you are powerful. You are great, you are great, you are great. You are brilliant, you are brilliant, you are brilliant. You are individual, you are individual, you are individual. You are unique, you are unique, you are unique. You are special, you are special, you are special. You are peaceful, you are peaceful, you are peaceful. You are quiet, you are quiet, you are quiet. You are thoughtful, you are thoughtful, you are thoughtful. You are appreciative, you are appreciative, you are appreciative. You are positive, you are positive, you are positive. You are inspiring, you are inspiring, you are inspiring. You are incredible, you are incredible, you are incredible. You are magnificent, you are magnificent, you are magnificent. You are amazing, you are amazing, you are amazing. You are so great, you are so great, you are so great. You have so many qualities, you have so many qualities, you have so many qualities.

I am positive, I am positive.

Magic Wand

Close your eyes and be very still. Breathe in and out slowly. Breathe in and breathe all the way out slowly and steadily. Imagine in front of you is a magic wand. See the wand sparkling in the sunlight. The magic wand is hovering in front of you. Watch it floating in mid air. Slowly reach out and take the magic wand. As soon as you hold it in your hands, you notice a ripple of energy pass from your fingers through your arm and all the way down your body. It is a pleasant feeling, like a jolt of excitement and you feel your hand quiver as you hold the magic wand. This is your own personal wand. It can cast all sorts of wonderful spells on you. You can't cast spells on anyone else. They would need to use their own magic wand. Your magic wand can cast a peace spell or a love spell or a joy spell. What spell would you like today? How would you like to feel? The spell is very powerful and will last all day. How would you like to feel for the rest of the day? Would you like to feel peaceful and calm and relaxed? Would you like to feel full of love? Would you like to feel full of happiness and joy? Choose which spell you would like. Once you have chosen your spell, stay very still and take a deep breath and breathe out slowly while you say 'Transformus!' Wave the magic wand in the air three times and watch the sparks of magic fly out of the tip of the wand. These sparks sprinkle all over you. You feel a tingle of energy inside as the magic spell touches you. Stay still and feel your whole body tingling as the magic spreads all the way down to your toes. Breathe in, breathe out. Breathe in, breathe out. Breathe in, breathe out. You feel the effects of the magic instantly. You feel happy that you are able to change so quickly.

I have the power to change, I have the power to change.

Cinema Screen

Close your eyes and be very still. Breathe in and out slowly. Breathe in and breathe all the way out slowly and steadily. Imagine in front of you is a huge cinema screen. This is a special cinema screen where you can watch films of your life. On this screen you can create the life you would like to lead. How would you like life to be at home? How would you like life to be in school? What would you like life to be in the future when you get older? Before you switch on the screen, become very still and silent inside. You are going to create a positive picture of your life. It is very important that you prepare yourself by becoming still and calm. Now switch on the cinema screen. You see lots of colors and pictures in front of you. You can see your name in big letters. This is the film of your life. Use your thoughts to put whatever you would like in your life up on the screen. If you would like more happiness, see images of all the people you know smiling and laughing and being joyful. If you want more love and kindness in your life, see your friends and family being kind and loving to one another. See them hugging and being gentle and caring. If you want more fun and creativity in your life, see yourself writing and painting and drawing. You see yourself dancing and playing games and playing outside in nature. If you would like to be more confident, you see yourself walking into a room standing tall and looking so cool and confident. You see yourself trying out new things and finding everything easy. If you want more luck and positivity in your life, you see yourself being lucky and fortunate. Happy surprises come your way and you feel positive and optimistic about life. Whatever you would like in your life, create it on this magic cinema screen and watch it slowly happen in real life. Everything starts with your thoughts. If you can have positive thoughts, you can attract positive things in your life. Stay for a few moment watching the positive images on the cinema screen.

I am positive, I am positive

Golden Heart

Close your eyes and be very still. Breathe in and out slowly. Breathe in and breathe all the way out slowly and steadily. Let your whole body become calm and relaxed. Let go and relax. Let go and relax. That's right. Just relax. Now concentrate on the point in the very centre of your chest. Imagine there is a tiny ball of the golden light in your chest. Stay very still. Can you feel it? Feel this ball of light getting brighter and brighter as you concentrate on it. Feel the ball of light getting bigger and bigger and bigger. As it grows it is getting stronger and stronger. Feel the light fill up your entire chest. You feel your heart filling up with so much love. Take in a deep breath and breathe in love. Breathe out love into the room. Breathe in love, breathe out love, breathe in love and breathe out love. Each time you breathe love, you feel the ball of light getting strong and bigger. Now think about who you would like to send this ball of love to. Is there someone who you know might need some extra help and love at this time? It could be someone you know or someone you don't know. It could be a child or adult or even an animal. It could even be a whole area or city or part of the world. Imagine there is a thin ray of light coming out of the ball of light and it moves gently through the air. The light is glowing. It touches the heart of the person you are sending love to. Watch as the light starts to grow in their chest. If you are sending light to an area, you see the ball of light getting bigger and bigger in that area. The light is getting stronger and stronger and brighter and brighter. Watch the person or people smile as the light of love fills their whole body. You notice them smile as they become full of the light of love. Notice how you are connected to that person or area. See how you are connected by the invisible thread of love. You are connected to every person by love. You are connected to every animal by love. You are connected to everything by love. Love is the thread that binds everything and everyone together.

I am love, I am love.

Campfire

Close your eyes and be very still. Breathe in and out slowly.
Breathe in and breathe all the way out slowly and steadily.

Imagine you are in the woods at night. You are not alone but surrounded by all your family and friends and those who are close to you. In the clearing you can see a campsite has been set up. In the centre of the campsite is a fire. You move toward the warmth and sit down. Spend a few moments watching the fire crackle as you stare into the flames. Watch the flames dance in the air. Enjoy watching the flames leaping and flickering. Enjoy listening to the fire spit and crackle. Feel the warmth of the fire on your face and the cool night air all around you. Feel your muscles relaxing and warming up, becoming more and more still. Watch the fire flash and flare. Enjoy the flames' quiver. Relax as the fire blazes and sparks in the night. Become aware of the night and the sounds of the night. Can you hear the owls hooting? Can you hear the foxes calling? Can you hear the scratching and furrowing mice in the undergrowth? Can you hear the flapping of bats in the trees? What can you hear? Stay very still and concentrate on your breathing as you listen to the sounds of the wood. As you watch the fire, become aware of the smell of burning wood. Watch the orb of flames gleam in the moonlight. Enjoy the heat as you feel your whole body warming and relaxing. You can notice the smoke coming up from the fire. The flames are swirling and rolling like a curling snake in the air. Watch the patterns form in the midnight sky. Slowly you start to notice that the smoke is forming words and shapes. What can you see in the smoke? Do you see words and pictures? Spend a few moments watching the fire snap and crack, flash and flare, roar and bellow. Enjoy the feeling of warmth on your body. Watch the words coming from the smoke. Stay here for a while watching the embers glow and gleam. You feel so relaxed and calm.

I am calm and relaxed, I am calm and relaxed.

Waterfall

Close your eyes and be very still. Breathe in and out slowly. Breathe in and breathe all the way out. Imagine you are in the mountains. The air is so fresh and invigorating. Take in a deep breath of mountain air and breathe out slowly. In front of you, you see a beautiful waterfall. The water looks wonderful as it rushes down from the tallest mountain. It is glistening in the sunshine. You feel the warmth of the sunshine on your face and body. Go up to the water and step into the wonderful waterfall. The waterfall takes away all your stress, anxiety, worry, and all your angry and frustrated thoughts and feelings. Stand under the powerful stream and feel the pure water gushing over your whole body. It feels cleansing and clearing. As you stand under the water, you feel as if all your negative emotions are flowing away with the water. The water carries them all away. Feel the thoughts of upset and anxiety melting away from your head as the water washes over you. Feel the water flowing all the way from your head down to your back and arms and away into the pool. Feel the cooling water wash all over you. You feel refreshed. You feel clean and clear. You feel fresh. Stay as still as you can and allow the cleansing water to take away all your negative thoughts. It feels so wonderful. It feels so cleansing and invigorating. You almost feel like a new person. You feel fresh and alive. You feel excited. All your sad thoughts and feelings are washed away. They have flowed out of you.

I am positive, I am positive.

Chill Pill

Close your eyes and be very still. Breathe in and out slowly. Breathe in and breathe all the way out slowly and steadily. I stay calm and peaceful. I stay calm and peaceful. When something happens, I do my best not to be affected. I am in control of my emotions. I know how to be calm and peaceful. I know how to be calm and peaceful. I know that anger does not make me feel any better. It does not make me feel good about myself. I know that anger does not bring me peace. I learn how to feel calm inside. I know how to feel cool. I allow my head and my mind to feel cool. I slowly count to 10 and as I count, I feel peace. I feel peaceful. I feel peaceful. I fill my body with these feelings of peace. All agitated and irritable thoughts are slowly melting away. I feel peaceful. I feel a sense of calm and a great sense of achievement that I can change my thoughts and feelings in such a short time. When I feel I am getting hot-tempered, I take time out to reassess the situation. I use the power of my mind to become calm and peaceful. I know how to be level-headed and not to react too quickly. Like a great martial artist, I know that power is in stillness and strength is in not reacting. I stay steady and firm and in control. I know that I am great and I do not need to use anger to get what I want. I do not need to use anger to control situations. Anger is not the answer and I know in the long run, it causes more problems for myself and others. I can show others that I am in control. I stay still and feel my inner power and strength. I know how to breathe to calm myself down. I learn to take in a slow breath and breathe out slowly. I learn to direct this energy into positive things. I know how to stand up for myself without using force. I have inner strength and I choose to exercise inner strength by not getting angry. I know how to speak without getting annoyed. I know how to deal with situations in a calm and balanced way. I am calm and balanced. I do not need to lash out. I find other ways to express myself. I am OK. I choose to be

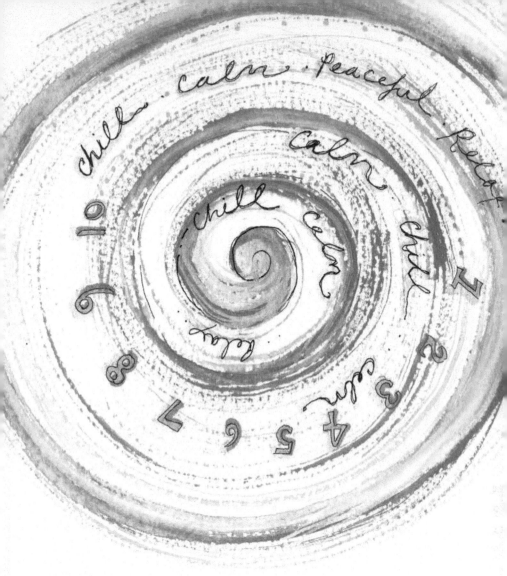

balanced and cool-headed. It feels better when I act with coolness. I feel at peace inside. I enjoy this feeling of peace. It feels good to be peaceful and cool and calm and serene. I feel calm and peaceful. I feel calm and peaceful. I feel calm and peaceful. I spend a few moments enjoying this peace and calm and thinking about how I can increase it daily.

I am at peace, I am at peace.

Melting Chocolate

Close your eyes and be very still. Breathe in and out slowly. Breathe in and breathe all the way out slowly and steadily. Imagine you are made of chocolate and lying in the warm sunshine. Very slowly, you are going to melt. Feel your right hand melting. Your right hand is heavy and relaxed. Your right arm is now melting and becoming heavy and relaxed. Feel your left hand melting. It is heavy and relaxed. Feel your left arm melting. Your left arm is heavy and relaxed. Feel your right foot. Your right foot melting. It is heavy and relaxed. Feel your right leg melting. Your right leg is heavy and relaxed. Feel your left foot melting into the ground. Your left foot is heavy and relaxed. Feel your left leg melting into the ground. Your left leg is heavy and relaxed. Feel your stomach softening and melting. Your stomach is heavy and relaxed. Take in a deep breath and breathe out, relaxing your stomach. Feel your lower back melting into the ground. Your lower back is heavy and relaxed. Take in a deep breath and breathe out, relaxing your lower back. Feel your whole spine becoming relaxed and melting. Feel your shoulders. Your shoulders are melting and becoming heavy and relaxed. Take in a deep breath and breathe out, relaxing your shoulders. Feel your neck. Your neck is melting and becoming heavy and relaxed. Take in a deep breath and breathe out, relaxing your neck. Feel your throat. Your throat is melting. Take in a deep breath and breathe out, relaxing your throat. Feel your head. Your head is melting and becoming heavy and relaxed. Feel your face relaxing and melting. Relax the your forehead, your right eyebrow, your left eyebrow, your right eye, your left eye, your right cheek, your left cheek, your right ear, your left ear, your right nostril, your left nostril, your upper lip, your lower lip, and your chin. Take a deep breath in and breathe out, relaxing your head as it melts. Stay there for a while, breathing deeply and enjoying the feeling of softness and deep relaxation.

I am relaxed, I am relaxed.

Television Screen

Close your eyes and be very still. Breathe in and out slowly. Breathe in and breathe all the way out slowly and steadily. Imagine you have your own television screen. This screen shows only positive words. The television screen is there to make you feel joyful and happy. Switch on the screen and sit comfortably in front. You see a series of positive words and bright colors on the screen. You see the word JOY. What does joy mean to you? How does joy feel? The next word is LAUGHTER. How does laughter make you feel? Do you enjoy laughing? You see the word KINDNESS. What is real kindness? Are you kind? How does kindness feel? How does it feel when someone is kind to you? You see the word HAPPY. What is real happiness to you? Do you feel happy? How does happiness feel inside? Do you like feeling happy? You see the word FRIENDSHIP. What does friendship mean? Are you are good friend? Do you have many friends? How do you make friends? You see the word CONFIDENCE. What is confidence? Do you have confidence? How does it feel to be confident? You see all these positive words moving on the screen. Just looking at them make you feel happy and positive. Now see the screen shrinking in size. The TV screen is getting smaller and smaller and smaller until it is only the size of a postage stamp. It is so tiny you can put it somewhere safe to keep it for whenever you need it. Where did you put the screen? Whenever you need to see some positive words, you just have to get your tiny screen out and watch it for a while and think about some positive words.

I am positive, I am positive.

Health Drink

Close your eyes and be very still. Imagine you have a glass of health drink. As you drink the special drink, say the following words to yourself, 'I am healthy, I enjoy being healthy. Every part of my body is healthy. I feel vital and alive. I eat healthy food. I love the taste of crunchy fruit and vegetables. I enjoy fresh healthy foods because I feel that they make a positive difference to my body. I take in all the nutrients I need to enjoy a healthy life. I drink water. I enjoy drinking water to keep my body in good condition. I feel the water flushing through me, clearing my body. I feel so healthy and alive when I drink water. I enjoy sleep. I allow my body to get enough rest. I feel fresh and energized when I have enough rest and sleep. I enjoy the freshness of outdoors. I enjoy breathing in fresh air. I fill my lungs with fresh air. I feel the fresh air oxygenating my blood. I love breathing in fresh outdoor air. I love exercising and feel vibrant when I exercise. I love running and playing sports, cycling, swimming and dancing. I enjoy moving my limbs. I am full of energy. I love exercising because it makes me feel energetic. I feel great when I exercise. I enjoy spending a few moments in the sunshine. I love taking in the warmth and energy of the sun. The sun makes me feel happy and alive. I am healthy. I am healthy. I am strong. My body feels strong. I am able to fight off infections easily. Everyday I make choices to stay healthy. Each day, I make a promise to myself to choose the right things for my body. I choose to eat healthily, drink water, get enough sleep, breathe in fresh air, exercise and take in some sunshine. I love myself when I make right and healthy choices for my body. I have more and more respect for myself. I do these things because I love and respect myself and I want to remain healthy so I can have a great life. These are the simple choices that are going to give me a great and vibrant life. I feel so grateful for my body. I know that feeling happy inside has a positive effect on my body. My body knows how to heal itself. My body is amazing. I just have to use my mind and think healthy thoughts and my health instantly improves. I appreciate my body, I accept my body just the way that it is. I know that through positive healthy choices, I can make my body work even better. I love my body and know that it is amazing. I choose to do good things for my body.

I am healthy, I am healthy.

Worry Balloons

Close your eyes and be very still. Breathe in and out slowly. Breathe in and breathe all the way out slowly and steadily. Now think about your worries. Imagine by your side is a balloon. Hold the balloon and imagine that you are writing all your worries on the balloon. When you have written down all your worries, imagine that the balloon is floating up into the sky. Enjoy watching the balloon as it floats gently into the air. As it rises, feel as if your troubles are slowly disappearing. Feel as if your worries are moving further and further away and you are feeling more and more relaxed and free. Enjoy this feeling of freedom. See if you can feel more and more peaceful. Breathe in and breathe out. Breathe in and breathe out. Now, gently put your hands on your stomach. As you take in a breath watch what happens to your hands and watch again as you breathe out. Breathe in, and breathe out. Breathe in and breathe out. As you breathe in, you may notice your hand moving up as your stomach rises and as you breathe out, your hands fall down again. You are breathing deep into the diaphragm. This is very calming and restful. Breathe in and breathe out. Breathe in and breathe out. Breathe in and breathe out. Each time you breathe out, feel as if you are breathing your worries away. Breathe in and breathe out and send the worries far away into the distance. Breathe in and breathe out, sending the worries away from you. Stay still and enjoy the feeling of a few worry-free moments. At this time, you do not need to worry about anything. Just imagine that you are free from worries for just a few moments. And now, ask yourself, how worried do you feel? Do you feel less worried now? Continue to enjoy the feeling of calm and tranquillity you have created.

I am calm, I am calm.

Secret Door

Close your eyes and be very still. Breathe in and out slowly. Breathe in and breathe all the way out slowly and steadily. Imagine you are standing at a secret door. Behind the door there are wonderful things. This door leads to all things positive and happy. You put your ear up against the door and you can hear wonderful positive words which make you feel amazing. Listen to the words telling you how special you are, 'You can choose to be special. You can choose to be brilliant. You can choose to feel good. You can choose to change. You can choose to be super. You can choose to be happy. You can choose to improve each day. You can choose to have more joy. You can choose to be positive. You can choose to be strong. You can choose to be resourceful. You can choose to be courageous. You can choose to be successful. You can choose to be calm. You can choose to be confident. You can choose to succeed. You can choose to recognize your strengths and talents. You can choose to be confident inside and out. You can choose to learn from life. You can choose to appreciate yourself. You can choose to accept yourself. You can choose to believe in yourself. You can choose to be resilient. You can choose to be brave. You can choose to be the best you can be. You can choose to be brilliant. You can choose to make positive choices. You can choose to be amazing. You can choose to be awesome. You can choose to love yourself. You can choose to be a special individual. You can choose to be different. You can choose to do your best. You can choose to be strong. You can choose to believe in yourself.' Stay by the door for as long as you can, listening to the special words that make you feel great.

I believe in myself, I believe in myself.

Happy Place

Close your eyes and be very still. Breathe in and out slowly. Breathe in and breathe all the way out slowly and steadily. Now, imagine that you are sitting on a big comfy chair that you can take anywhere you wish. You could take it to a shady part of a wood or forest, or a beach or to an open field. Take your chair far, far away. Maybe it is at the top of a mountain or by a river or even in outer space. Take your chair to a place where you are alone and feel safe. This is your special happy place. You cannot be disturbed in your happy place and there are no dangers so you do not have to be afraid. Everything here is friendly and you are safe. Say to yourself, 'I am safe. I am secure. I am comfortable. I am safe. I am secure. I am comfortable.' Now you have created this special, safe, happy place, look around and notice the colors and sounds in your happy place. You feel like smiling as you start to feel happy. You are free to come back to this special place whenever someone is hurting you or being nasty to you. You can come here whenever you feel you want to be safe and secure and alone. In your imagination, see if you can give yourself a big hug. Stay very still and imagine that you are being surrounded in a wonderful and huge hug. Keep your eyes closed and feel that you are swirling around in a warm, friendly and loving hug. Give yourself a big hug. Hold this hug for as long as you can. Remind yourself that you are your best friend and you can give yourself a hug whenever you need. Breathe in love, breathe out love. Breathe in love, breathe out love. Breathe in love, breathe out love. Stay for a few moments feeling the love inside your heart and enjoying being in your happy place.

I am happy, I am happy.

Crossroads

Close your eyes and be very still. Breathe in and out slowly. Breathe in and breathe all the way out slowly and steadily. Imagine you are looking at a map. On the map are all the different roads that you can take. It feels a bit confusing as you are not sure which way to go and what to do. Which direction would you like to take? Which direction would serve you best? Which option would make you feel good about yourself? Which decision would help improve the situation? Stay very still and see if you can get a feeling for which way you should go. Imagine that you are walking along a path and you come to some cross-roads. Stand at the crossroads and think about which path to take. All of a sudden, you notice the wisest, kindest person or creature you can imagine walking up to you. They ask you some questions. Where would you like to go? What would you like to achieve? What is your goal? What would you like in your life? What is stopping you getting these things? Why are you confused? The wise creature or person invites you to sit down under a huge old oak tree. Lean back against the trunk and feel the warm sun on your face and the warm breeze on your skin. You feel quiet. Think about these questions. Stay quiet and still and think about where you would like to go, what you would like to achieve, what your goals are, what you would like in your life, what is stopping you and why you are confused. Stay still for a while and think. Now, turn to the wise creature or person and ask a question. Stay still as you listen to the answer. Stay as quiet and as still as you can listening to the answer. And now ask yourself on a scale of one to ten, how confused do you feel? Spend some time enjoying the feeling of calm and focussed thoughts you have created.

I am wise, I am wise.

Confidence Boost

Close your eyes and be very still. Breathe in and out slowly. Breathe in and breathe all the way out slowly and steadily. As you are breathing gently and calmly, become aware of the different parts of your body. Start with your feet and legs. Become aware of the hard or soft surface below you. Become aware of the stillness in your legs. Become aware of your stomach. Release any tension by gently letting go and relaxing. Become aware of the areas you need to relax. Draw your attention to your chest and release any tightness as you continue to breathe in and breathe out slowly. Bring your awareness to your spine. Imagine there is a light going up from the base of your spine to the top of your head. As you become aware of this light, you feel yourself growing taller and taller. As you feel yourself growing taller, you start to feel more confident and self-assured. You feel strong and brave. Repeat to yourself, 'I am strong and brave and in control. I am strong and brave and in control. I am strong and brave and in control.' Bring your attention to your head. Feel as though your head is full of light. Feel your head is full of confidence. Feel the light all the way through your spine and into your head. Feel the golden thread pulling you up, making you feel taller and taller. As you grow taller, you feel more and more full of confidence. Say to yourself, 'I am confident. I am confident. I am confident. I am confident.'

I am calm and in control, I am calm and in control.

Cloak of Protection

Close your eyes and be very still. Breathe in and out slowly. Breathe in and breathe all the way out slowly and steadily. Imagine that you are wearing an invisible cloak. This cloak is surrounding you and protecting you from any harm. If ever anyone says something unkind, then any negative or hurtful words just bounce off the cloak. Imagine for a moment, some unkind bullies saying some nasty words and watch and feel as the words bounce off the cloak. Spend a moment watching as the words bounce off the cloak. Notice how strong you feel as you are left unhurt and unharmed by their nastiness. It is almost as if there is a wall between you and the bullies. No one can harm you. Imagine yourself feeling so confident that you can stand up for yourself and say NO to the bullies. Imagine how tall and strong you feel. Imagine how brave inside you feel. Imagine how confident you feel. Imagine how courageous you feel. Imagine how good you feel about yourself. Imagine the feeling you get when you show that you are not hurt by their taunts and their words. Imagine how great you feel when you know that you are in control. Spend a few moments seeing yourself standing tall, surrounded by the cloak and saying NO to the bullies. Repeat to yourself in your mind, 'I am strong, I am brave and I am in control. I am strong, I am brave and I am in control. I am strong, I am brave and I am in control.'

I am protected, I am protected.

River

Close your eyes and be very still. Breathe in and out slowly. Breathe in and out slowly. Breathe in and breathe all the way out slowly and steadily. Imagine you are lying in a boat floating on the river. Allow your body to relax as you feel the warm sun on your body. You can hear the gentle ripples of the water. You feel the boat rocking from side to side as you go into a deep relaxation. Feel your feet relaxing. Let your toes completely relax and become soft. Let this feeling spread gently through your feet. Now squeeze your legs and gently let them go. Feel all the tension in your legs being released as they become relaxed and soft. Squeeze the muscles in your tummy and let go completely. Stretch your back as long as you can and relax. Can you feel your back sinking into the boat? Now let your shoulders and neck become soft, as all the tension melts away. Squeeze your arms as tight as you can and let them go. Allow your arms to feel heavy as they sink into the boat. Squeeze your fingers into a tight fist and now uncurl them slowly and let them relax. Scrunch your face into a tiny ball and let go and relax. Let your head completely relax. Relax your eyes, your ears, your cheeks, your forehead. Become completely still and relaxed. Feel the warm sun on your face and body as you rock from side to side in the boat. Stay there for a few more moments, enjoying the feeling of being completely relaxed. Repeat to yourself in your head, I am calm, I am relaxed, I am cool, I am quiet, I feel peaceful, I am still, I am soft, I am gentle, I am warm, I am relaxed, I am relaxed.

I am relaxed, I am relaxed.

Dinosaurs

Close your eyes and be very still. Breathe in and out slowly. Breathe in and breathe all the way out slowly and steadily. Imagine you are on Jurassic Island. All around you there are giant green ferns and palms. This is the land of the dinosaurs. You notice some dinosaur footprints and decide to follow them. The footprints take you through the forest and over the hills to a huge cave in the rocks. Behind the rocks you see a family of dinosaurs. They are kind and friendly. You see Calmasaurus who is quiet and calm, Happisaurus who is smiling brightly and Relaxasuarus who is relaxing on the ground. Go up to Calmasaurus. You notice how peaceful and relaxed he is. He is breathing deeply. Follow his breathing. He is breathing in and out so slowly and softly. As you breathe in and out, you feel calm and quiet, like Calmasaurus. Breathe in calm, breathe out calm. Say to yourself, 'I am calm. I am calm.' Happisaurus comes to greet you. He is full of fun and energy. He has a friendly face with a big smile. He wants to jump and play. He wants to run and skip and he wants you to join in. Have fun playing and running with Happisaurus. How does this make you feel? Do you feel a tingling feeling of happiness in your fingers and toes? After a while, you start to feel tired and notice Relaxasaurus lying peacefully on the ground. Go up to Relaxasaurus and lie down with your head on her tummy. She is breathing softly and steadily. As she breathes in, your head rises gently and as she breathes out, your head falls again. She is warm and cosy and you feel so calm and relaxed. Breathe in, breathe out. Breathe in, breathe out. Say to yourself, 'I am calm and relaxed. I am calm and relaxed.' As you lie there, feel the warm sunshine on your body and face. Feel the warm sunshine on your body and face. Feel the warmth from Relaxasurus's body. You feel warm and safe. You enjoy lying on the warm cushion. The cushion is soft and warm. Your body feels soft and warm. You are calm and relaxed. You are calm and relaxed. You are calm and relaxed. You feel totally safe.

I am calm, I am calm

Under the Sea

Close your eyes and be very still. Imagine you are sitting in a boat out at sea. You feel excited because you are about to go on a diving adventure in the sea. Put on your protective diving suit, mask and breathing equipment and jump into the water. It feels warm as the sun is very bright. The sea is calm and clear. Dive down into the open water. Listen to your breathing. You can hear the muffled sound of air as you breathe in and out through your diving equipment. You can hear the sound of bubbles escaping from your regulator. It feels wonderful to be breathing under-water, you feel so alive and free. Your whole body feels weightless as you drift through the ocean. Feel how relaxed your body is. Your limbs are relaxed and it feels as though there is space in between your joints. Everything is fun and free. Look around and see the sunlight shimmering on the water. Notice the bubbles glinting like tiny stars in the expanse of the ocean. See the rays of the sun beaming down through the water like rainbow lasers. It looks beautiful. Feel yourself drifting, being carried by the currents. Feel your whole body being held by the water. Look around and see shoals of multi-colored fish swimming past you. They are darting and diving. Some larger fish swim slowly past you. Dolphins come to greet you. Can you hear their high-pitched calls? The dolphins are playful and friendly. They love to play. Dolphins are loving and joyful creatures who just like to be joyful and loving all day long. Enjoy playing with the dolphins for a while. Just float there gently as they dip and dive past you. They are so loving and gentle. Feel how loving and gentle these dolphins are. Feel how playful and friendly they are. As you float in the water, spend some moments imagining how life would be if everyone you knew was as kind and loving as a dolphin. Imagine what your life would be like if you were kind and loving to everyone you knew. What would it be like to be more friendly and caring towards others? Think about what you are going to do when you get back from your diving adventure to be more kind and loving. Enjoy floating as you breathe in love and breathe out joy. Breathe in love and breathe out joy.

I am joyful, I am joyful.

Wishing Chair

Close your eyes and be very still. Breathe in and out slowly.
Breathe in and breathe all the way out slowly and steadily.

Imagine you are sitting on a wishing chair. The chair is soft against your skin. The cushions are large and made of feathers. You feel your whole body sinking into the soft feather cushions. Feel yourself relaxing and letting go. Breathe in, relax, breathe out, relax. Breathe in, relax, breathe out, relax. This is a very special chair. It is the wishing chair. Whenever you have a problem, you can just sit in this chair and you can wish your problem away with some very special magic words. If someone has upset you, or you are sad about a situation or if a friend has fallen out with you, you just have to sit in the chair and wish the problem away. The chair is magic and you just have to repeat the magic words over and over and over and over again. Would you like to know the magic words? Are you ready? Make yourself comfortable in the chair and become as still as you possibly can. Feel yourself being still and quiet. Say very quietly in your mind, 'I'm sorry, please forgive me. I love you. Thank you.' The words might not make sense to you at first but you just have to know that they hold special magic powers. Just by repeating the words over and over and over and over again, the problem and hurt or bad feeling will melt away and you will start to feel peaceful and joyful. Breathe in and say, 'I'm sorry'. Breathe out and say, 'please forgive'. Breathe in and say, 'I love you'. Breathe out and say, 'thank you'. Breathe in and say, 'I'm sorry'. Breathe out and say, 'please forgive'. Breathe in and say, 'I love you'. Breathe out and say, 'thank you'. Breathe in and say, 'I'm sorry'. Breathe out and say, 'please forgive'. Breathe in and say, 'I love you'. Breathe out and say, 'thank you'. Continue to sit in the Wishing Chair repeating the magic words over and over and over and over again, as slow as you can. Notice how the magic works inside you as you repeat them.

I can change, I can change.

Magical Microphone

Close your eyes and be very still. Breathe in and out slowly. Breathe in slowly and relax. Imagine you are holding a microphone. This is a magical microphone. Whatever positive things you say into the microphone, they come true in your life. The microphone has an echo and so let the sound reverberate through the room and in your body and mind. I am amazing, amazing, amazing. I am athletic, athletic, athletic. I am adventurous, adventurous, adventurous. I am an achiever, an achiever, an achiever. I am adored, adored, adored. I am attractive, attractive, attractive. I am active, active, active. I am awesome, awesome, awesome. I am artistic, artistic, artistic. I am brilliant, brilliant, brilliant. I am beautiful, beautiful, beautiful. I am balanced, balanced, balanced. I am brave, I am bright, I am creative, I am colorful, I am calm, I am confident, I am cool, I am considerate, I am clever, I am courageous, I am clear, I am capable, I am caring, I am determined, I am energetic, I am exciting, I am enthusiastic, I am extraordinary, I am free, I am fun, I am friendly, I am funny, I am fabulous, I am fantastic, I am focussed, I am fortunate, I am forgiving, I am fine, I am great, I am grateful, I am generous, I am gentle, I am happy, I am healthy, I am helpful, I am imaginative, I am intelligent, I am joyful, I am loving, I am lucky, I am lovely, I am light, I am open, I am positive, I am powerful, I am peaceful, I am precious, I am playful, I am patient, I am popular, I am quiet, I am radiant, I am relaxed, I am resourceful, I am responsible, I am respectful, I am resilient, I am supportive, I am sincere, I am sunny, I am serene, I am successful, I am skillful, I am a star, I am super, I am sweet, I am safe, I am self-confident, I am talented, I am terrific, I am trustworthy, I am thoughtful, I am tranquil, I am truthful, I am unique, I am valuable, I am victorious, I am vibrant, I am wonderful, I am wealthy, I am worthy, I am a winner, I am wondrous. Stay still as you let the words from the microphone

echo all the way around the room and into your body and mind.
I am unique, I am unique.

Traffic Lights

Close your eyes, be very still. Imagine you have an amazing traffic light system inside your body. These lights can change color and so help you change your moods and feelings. First of all imagine your whole body turning a strong and vibrant red. See this strong red light up your body until it is full of red light. You are radiating red light. See this red light. Be the red light. This red light is full of strength and courage. Send this strong red light out to the world. Be strong and courageous. You can use this red light when you need to feel strong and courageous. Now feel the red light fading and turning into a bright orange light. See this orange light growing stronger until your body is full of orange light. You are radiating orange light. See this orange light. Be the orange light. This orange light is full of fun and joy. Send this joyful orange light out to the world. Be joyful. You can use this orange light when you need to feel joyful. Now feel the orange light fading and turning into a soft yellow light. See this soft yellow light growing stronger until your body is full of yellow light. You are radiating yellow light. See this yellow light. Be the yellow light. This yellow light is full of confidence and power. Send this soft yellow light out to the world. Be powerful and confident. You can use this yellow light when you need to feel powerful and confident. Now feel the yellow light fading and turning into a green light. See this green light growing stronger until your body is full of green light. You are radiating green light. See this green light. Be the green light. This green light is full of love and friendship. Send this green light out to the world. Be loving. You can use this green light when you need to feel loving and friendly. Now feel the green light fading and turning into a soft blue light. See this soft blue growing stronger until your body is full of blue light. You are radiating blue light. See this blue light. Be the blue light. This blue light is full of peace

100

and harmony. Send this soft blue light out to the world. Be peaceful. You can use this blue light when you need to feel peaceful. Now feel the blue light fading and turning into an indigo light. See this indigo light growing stronger until your body is full of indigo light. You are radiating indigo light. See this indigo light. Be the indigo light. This indigo light is full of creativity. Send this indigo light out to the world. Be creative. You can use this indigo light when you need to feel creative. Now feel the indigo light fading and turning into a bright violet light. See this bright violet light growing stronger until your body is full of violet light. You are radiating violet light. See this violet light. Be the violet light. This violet light is full of freedom and lightness. Send this bright violet light out to the world. Be blissful. Be light. You can use this violet light when you need to feel light and free. Now stay still and experiment changing the lights. You can change the color of your light whenever you wish.

I am light, I am light.

Space Ship

Close your eyes and be very still. Imagine you are in a space ship that takes you up into the sky, past the clouds and into outer space. You are excited about your space adventure and wonder which planet you will visit today. Feel yourself whizzing through space. You feel so light and weightless. You are traveling faster than the speed of light. Feel yourself soaring upwards. You feel light and weightless. The space ship starts to slow down as you reach your first stop. It looks like a very strange planet. Where are you? When you have come to a stop, open the door and step out. Feel your whole body is weightless as you bounce lightly on the planet. It is a wonderful feeling being weightless. You feel light and free. You notice the surface of the planet is rough. You see crags and crevices. Bounce lightly over the rocks. You see hidden caves and wonder who lives in the caves. You hear a sound. It is very unusual and you have never heard anything quite like it before. It seems like someone is speaking in a whizzing and whirring way. You notice a friendly alien come out to greet you. He is very colorful. Can you see what he looks like? How many eyes does your alien have? How many legs and arms does he have? Your friendly alien greets you with a handshake and a strange alien greeting. You feel quite safe with him. He offers to take you around his homeland. The alien is so chatty. He doesn't stop talking. You don't understand his language, but you still seem to understand what he is saying. He shows you his family and his pets. They all look so strange and unfamiliar to you, but they are kind and generous. You probably look very strange and unfamiliar to them but they like you because you are polite and friendly. Now it is time for you to leave the planet. You say goodbye to your friend. You realize that although this alien is so different and sounds so different, is a different color and shape and lives in a different home, you can still be friends and respect each other. The alien has shown you that no matter how different

others look on the outside, there is always something good to be found inside. You feel happy with yourself that you have learnt to be respectful of someone else's life and learnt to accept them for who they are and not mind how different they are.

I am respectful, I am respectful.

Jungle Adventure

Close your eyes and be very still. Breathe in and out slowly. Breathe in slowly and relax. Breathe in and breathe all the way out slowly and steadily. Imagine you are in a jungle. Close your eyes and listen to the sounds of the jungle. You can hear the monkeys chatting and the hyenas laughing, the parrots squawking, big cats roaring, the elephants trumping, and the rhinos snorting. The jungle is quite a noisy place. The jungle is a rich place, filled with color and activity, energy and vibrance. There is always something new to hear and something new to see each moment. Even in the middle of the night when most animals are asleep, there is noise and activity. Stay very still and watch the animals around you. Can you see the elephants and buffalo playing in the mud? Can you see the tigers and jaguars stretching out in the sunshine? Can you see the monkeys playing high in the trees? Can you see the giraffe peacefully munching leaves? Can you see the parrots flying? Can you see the multi-colored butterflies fluttering all around you? Can you see the green frogs jumping in the underground? Can you see the crocodiles sloping off into the water? The jungle is such an incredible place. You feel in awe looking at the variety of creatures all around you. Each animal knows its job and is part of the rich tapestry of this beautiful place. The jungle vibrates with energy and color. It is a patchwork of vitality and life. And now stay totally still. Take a deep breath and breathe all the way out. Breathe in and breathe out. Breathe in and breathe out. Feel yourself becoming more and more still in the jungle as the animals move around you. The more still you can be, the more you can enjoy the sights and sounds of the jungle. Continue to breathe in and out, enjoying watching and listening to the sounds of the jungle.

I am still, I am still.

Circus

Close your eyes and be very still. Breathe in and out slowly. Breathe in slowly and relax. Breathe in and breathe all the way out slowly and steadily. Imagine you are a talented circus performer. Who would you like to be? Would you like to be a tightrope walker balancing in the air? Would you like to be a trapeze artist swinging high into the air? Would you like to be a funny clown making people laugh? Would you like to be a juggler or an acrobat? What skill would you like to have? Imagine you are the tightrope walker. You are high up in the air, balancing on a thin wire. You have such brilliant focus and concentration. You are very patient and calm as you slowly walk across the wire. Can you feel how amazing it is to be far up in the air? Do you know how skilled you are to be so focussed and concentrated? You feel very proud of yourself for being so still and focussed inside. You feel proud that you have put in hours of practice to be so talented. Now imagine you are a trapeze artist. Feel yourself swinging high up into the air. Forwards and backwards, backwards and forwards. Feel the wind rush past your face as you fly through the air with such skill and agility. You are so light and full of energy. Inside you are very alert as you fly through the air with such ease. You feel proud of yourself that you are so agile and energetic. You feel so pleased that you are so flexible. You feel so proud that you have put in hours of practice to be so talented. Now imagine that you are a clown. As soon as you enter the ring, everyone laughs. You make everyone smile. You make others so happy and joyful. You know how to bring happiness to so many. You enjoy listening to the laughter and the clapping. Inside, you feel you proud and happy that you can bring happiness to so many. You feel so proud that you have put in hours of practice to be so talented. Now imagine you are a juggling stilt walker. You are so talented. You have good balance and concentration. You are able to balance and juggle at the same

time. It feels amazing being so high up and watching the colorful balls in the air. You feel so proud that you are so skilled and courageous. You feel so proud that you have put in hours of practice to be so talented. Which circus act was your favorite? Spend a few more moments performing your favorite act. Hear the audience roar with delight and applaud your talent loudly. You can hear them shout 'More! More!' and 'Bravo! Bravo!' You are a skilled and talented circus performer and it feels wonderful to share your skill with so many.

I am talented, I am talented.

Hot Air Balloon

Close your eyes and be very still. Breathe in and out slowly. Breathe in slowly and relax. Breathe in and breathe all the way out slowly and steadily. Imagine you are riding in a hot air ballon. It is sunset and the light is dusky. The balloon is rising softly into the air. You feel light and weightless as you rise higher into the sky. Your whole body feels light and free. All your muscles are relaxed and soft. You feel so happy and free as you glide upwards into the clouds. Feel the warm breeze on your face as you drift through the air. Your eyes feel relaxed. Your ears are relaxed. Your cheeks are soft and relaxed. Your mouth is soft and relaxed. You feel your hair blowing softly in the warm wind.

Look down below and see a hazy picture of rivers and patchwork fields. You see cornfields and green fields and fields of blue lavender and red poppies. You see gentle hills with tiny white sheep grazing peacefully. You can see the rivers lazily meandering through the countryside. The site is spectacular in the dusky sunset light. The sun is slowly setting. You can see a big orange-red orb slowly setting into the horizon. The sky is filled with colors. A spectacle of rainbow colors create a beautiful sunset. As the sun gently goes down, you feel the hot air balloon gently descend. It feels as if it is gliding downwards towards the ground. You feel as if you are gently flying downwards. It is floating downwards so softly. Breathe in and as you breathe out feel yourself getting closer to the ground. Breathe in, breathe out. Breathe in, breathe out.

I am free, I am free.

Wishing Well

Close your eyes and be very still. Breathe in and out slowly. Breathe in slowly and relax. Breathe in and breathe all the way out slowly and steadily. Imagine you are sitting in front of a wishing well. Look down into the wishing well as you make your special wishes. 'May I be filled with love and joy. May all those around me be filled with love and joy. May I be filled with loving kindness. May all those around me be filled with loving kindness. May I be filled with truth and honesty. May all those around me be filled with truth and honesty. May I be filled with hope. May all those around me be filled with hope. May I be filled with kindness and care towards all others. May all those around me be filled with kindness and care towards all others. May I love with all my heart. May those around me show love towards me. May I stay safe. May those around me stay safe. May I be healthy in my body and mind. May all those around me be healthy in mind and body. May I be successful. May all those around me be successful. May I enjoy my life. May all those around me enjoy their life. May I be patient and kind. May all those around me be patient and kind. May I show love to all creatures on earth. May all those around me show love to creatures on earth. May I always give thanks for everything I have. May all those around me give thanks. May I appreciate everything around me. May all those around me appreciate everything. May I be brilliant. May all those around me be brilliant. May I do my best. May all those around me do their best. May I be content. May all those around me be content. Stay near the wishing well and hold onto these positive feelings.

I am content, I am content.

**OUR STREET
BOOKS**

Our Street Books for children of all ages, deliver a potent mix of fantastic, rip-roaring adventure and fantasy stories to excite the imagination; spiritual fiction to help the mind and the heart grow; humorous stories to make the funny bone grow; historical tales to evolve interest; and all manner of subjects that stretch imagination, grab attention, inform, inspire and keep the pages turning. Our subjects include Non-fiction and Fiction, Fantasy and Science Fiction, Religious, Spiritual, Historical, Adventure, Social Issues, Humour, Folk Tales and more.

BEST THING *Ever*

Best Thing Ever is refreshing and genuine. It will help you claim your personal power and tune into your intuition. You will learn the real essence of love and the art of creating an invigorating life partnership."

—Sandra Yancey, the Founder of eWomenNetwork,
ABC Radio Show Host, Author, Movie Producer, and Speaker

As I started to read *Best Thing Ever*, I couldn't put it away. Written in a very friendly manner and truly a pleasure to read, it offers real value on every page. Sky Blossoms shares her own inspiring life story, along with other couples' happy relationship secrets. The book contains practical soul-search tools and is full of wisdom. Sky Blossoms reveals why it's not worth settling for less, how to invite the one into your life and how to extend the happiness of young love into a blissful lifetime.

—Dr. Irina Koles, M.D., M.H.M., Bestselling Author of
Taste of Thoughts: Improve Your Health and Whole Life

Invaluable tools, transformational processes, and real examples in *Best Thing Ever* make it a truly extraordinary book. Anyone who is looking for a genuine and lasting love relationship will benefit tremendously from its powerful and inspiring message!

—Michael S. Broder, Ph.D., Psychologist and Author of
Stage Climbing: The Shortest Path to Your Highest Potential

Brush aside the old confusing dogmas about relationships. *Best Thing Ever* sets the record straight on what it takes to create a happy intimate union. Sky Blossoms unravels the tangled mess in which we often find ourselves when it comes to relationships. I wish they taught these principles in school. It would prevent so many heartbreaks and divorces. *Best Thing Ever* is a treasure chest filled with practical advice; I loved it and I highly recommend it!

—Thomas Bähler, Composer, Producer, and Author of *Anything is Possible*

By artfully weaving practical wisdom with inspiring stories of successful love relationships (including her own!) in *Best Thing Ever*, Sky Blossoms shares a refreshing perspective on the meaning of commitment and how fun and deeply fulfilling a love relationship can be.

—Dina Proctor, Speaker, Coach and Author of *Madly Chasing Peace*

It's about time a book like this has been written! *Best Thing Ever* is a unique and reliable bridge between the realities of our daily life and ageless spiritual wisdom. With eloquent simplicity it spells out the fundamental principles upon which sincere and happy partnerships are formed. Sky Blossoms offers processes that are impressively effective and easy to follow. I highly recommend this book to all who are ready to welcome the magic of true love into their life.

—Anastasia Gorbunova, Ph.D., MBA, Experimental Psychology Researcher

Inspiring, motivating, and full of LOVE! After reading this book I have a deep understanding of love and how great it CAN be when we understand that every relationship is a mirror and a magical lesson for each individual. Throughout the book I laughed as stories were shared that we can all relate to about ex- boyfriends, situations, and relationships that were not meant to be for a lifetime but a stepping stone to creating an amazing life. Sky Blossoms shows you how to think differently about your love life in a way that brings out the best in each other…forever.

—Irene Tymczyszyn, Author and Speaker

A healthy and authentic intimate relationship creates a connected fortress in one's life. Sky Blossoms' art of storytelling takes us on a journey – a quest for wholeness – and unveils how to create that conscious connection within our heart and mind, adding more value and happiness to our experience. *Best Thing Ever* proves that a great partnership is natural – it is the moment when life starts to unfold before our very eyes. This book is nothing short of extraordinary. "The main recipient of your blessings is you." Personally, I love that!

—Dustin Heerkens, Lifestyle Coach, Explorer

BEST THING *Ever*

*Escape Disappointments and Drama
and Let True Love into Your Life*

SKY BLOSSOMS

NEW YORK

BEST THING *Ever*
Escape Disappointments and Drama and Let True Love into Your Life

ISBN 978-1-61448-583-4 paperback
ISBN 978-1-61448-584-1 eBook
ISBN 978-1-61448-585-8 audio
Library of Congress Control Number: 2013945227

Morgan James Publishing
The Entrepreneurial Publisher
5 Penn Plaza, 23rd Floor
New York City, New York 10001
(212) 655-5470 office • (516) 908-4496 fax
www.MorganJamesPublishing.com

Cartoons by
Nick Galifianakis

Tango Illustration by
Aleksey Vays

Cover Design by:
Sky Blossoms
Rachel Lopez
www.r2cdesign.com

Interior Design by:
Bonnie Bushman
bonnie@caboodlegraphics.com

Dedication

Dear reader, this book is a gift from my heart to yours. I dedicate it to your discovering happiness beyond your wildest dreams. The beauty of writing is in the music it creates in the reader's soul. May you become a living melody of Love.

Table of Contents

PART I:

In Search
of Answers

Let's Get Acquainted

*D*ear Friend,

The fact that you are holding this book in your hands is not an accident. Chances are it came as an answer to your questions and desires, whether you consciously voiced them or not. Have you ever dreamed about a romance that lasts a lifetime? Of finding that magical connection with the *one*? Did you want to be swept off your feet by overwhelming passion and excitement, but instead you've been heartbroken, disappointed, and discouraged to the point of questioning the whole idea of "Happily Ever After?" This book will show you a path to creating an extraordinary relationship in your life that far transcends traditional understanding.

A great relationship is like a state of health. According to The World Health Organization, "Health is a state of complete physical, mental, and social well-being and *not merely the absence of disease or infirmity.*" Likewise, a great relationship goes far beyond comfortable cohabitation, sexual compatibility, and shared interests. A healthy, intimate union means profound connection with another being on all levels—physical, intellectual, social, emotional, and

3

spiritual—which promotes greater fulfillment, happiness, self-expression, and evolution, for both partners.

Is such a relationship even attainable?

It is reachable just as much as the state of health. You can be an overall healthy person, which doesn't mean you don't get an occasional headache or a cold. We are not talking about absolute health, but rather a predominant state of wellness. In the same way, an extraordinary intimate union does not mean life without challenges or problems. Even the happiest couple will encounter a rare disagreement or an argument, which will inspire growth and even result in the deepening of the bond. However, the general and prevalent outcome of a healthy relationship is joy, and it is definitely achievable.

How can you create a healthy relationship and let true love into your life? What does it take?

- Have a powerful desire and understand your reasons for wanting a relationship—your "why"
- Break free from your own limitations and believe that you *can* create an extraordinary and lasting union
- Define your relationship vision
- Build a strong foundation within—gain your own balance
- Open your heart to the flow of love
- Become the honey—attract the love of your life

In this book, you will discover the secrets and practical steps that lead to an elated and lasting intimate union. *Best Thing Ever* will help you to crystallize your unique relationship vision, let go of the past, and create a strong and centered footing for your future. Together we will examine the common relationship myths that are responsible for many confusions and heartbreaks. You will learn to avoid standard pitfalls that guarantee disappointment. You will receive tools and learn powerful practices to prepare yourself for meeting the love of your life. We'll work through tips for choosing the right partner, and hone your ability to recognize the *one*.

Best Thing Ever is designed to inspire the fullness of life that you are to shine through and flow freely. If you are single, this book will show you the way to your inner freedom, which is necessary to make the bond with another person delightfully enjoyable. If you are involved with someone, this book will help you either to deepen your connection and invigorate your experience, or to release it and confidently move on.

Will these principles work for you?

You will learn proven techniques that are based on real-life results and draw on experiences of many successful couples. Whether you choose to apply them is up to you.

Is the author an expert?

I do not have a diploma in psychology or a PhD with which to impress you, nor do I care to be a licensed guru. I believe that results speak louder than fancy titles. My aim is to share my gifts and inspire happiness in you. I walked the path you are embarking on, and I have found the treasures you are seeking.

I come from a family of powerful healers, including my mother and both of her grandmothers. Their work was geared mainly toward physical healing. While I inherited many abilities from my female ancestors, my passions have always been communication and relationships. I studied psychology and human behavior for over fifteen years. I learned different modalities and techniques, from traditional mainstream teachings of the masters like Eric Berne, Carl Jung, and Viktor Frankl to metaphysical approaches like the Silva Mind Control Method, and Reiki healing. In time, I developed my own tools and practices. For years I was trying to figure out the best way to apply my talents. Finally, the path was revealed. Now I take my clients on a transformational journey from fear to love by helping them uncover and eradicate self-sabotaging patterns and open their hearts to the flow of love.

I graduated from a medical university as a dentist. Throughout the years of medical school classes, we were hardly ever taught *health*. What we learned were *diseases*. Many disorders exist, and learning them is complicated. Health, on the other hand, is the one and only state of wholesomeness. The same is true for relationships. There is an array of possible delusions, but true love is the one and only kind.

Unfortunately, no university teaches *health* or *love*. These cornerstones of life must be learned on one's own or from those who experience them on a daily basis. My relationship with my husband is everything I hoped for and much more—a real blessing, but not an accident. Similar to the science behind every great achievement, there is a formula to our success. And it is my privilege to share this formula with you.

We will not discuss dysfunctions or quick fixes. Instead, I invite you to mix in all the right ingredients to create a delicious and enduring intimate partnership. You don't need to twist into a pretzel, bend over backward, or act in a certain way. On the contrary, you will have to tune in to your very core and reveal your most authentic self. I will show you that creating a great personal relationship is rather easy. And it's truly the best thing ever.

Life Served on a Silver Platter

*A*llow me to share a part of my personal story to give you a better insight.

My journey started in Ukraine, where I was born and raised. My parents couldn't make ends meet, no matter how hard they tried. Out of desperation they took an opportunity and went to work abroad for nearly four years. Unfortunately they were unable to take me with them, and I was moved to another town to live with my grandparents. A teenager at the time, I entered into some of my darkest years suffering from depression and frequent suicidal thoughts.

Due to my parents' efforts, their financial situation significantly improved. My clothes were fancy, and I had many things that my classmates could only dream of. While my peers were showing admiration and high regard for material assets, I understood early on that human care and love were way more important than any tangible valuables. I was ready to give up all of that "stuff" for a chance to be with my parents.

Luckily, I didn't kill myself, and after reuniting with my mom and dad and moving back to my home city, life went back to normal for a while. I grew up, graduated from a medical university, and about a year later moved to the United States. The country of opportunities presented new challenges. Building my life from scratch, learning the language, and adapting to the new culture was tough. My survival skills were seriously tested. There were moments when I had no money for food and starved for a day. The battle to become a citizen took thirteen years. I worked to utter exhaustion, studying at nights, and I endured another seven years of not seeing my parents.

Nonetheless, these challenges were blessings, because hitting financial rock bottom taught me that it wasn't the end of the world, and I could survive almost anything. I learned humility and appreciation when I had to swallow my doctor's ego and be glad for the opportunity to paint a fence for six dollars an hour. Under the most desperate circumstances I felt a sense of purpose. My mantras were "If there is a will, there is a way" and "Whatever happens is for the better." Every time the next seemingly stalemate situation got resolved, I knew that I was not alone in this journey of life. The invisible force was guiding me. The wisdom and solutions were always available, if I had only listened.

At some level I always knew that life was not meant to be a struggle, and I was determined to find a path to consistent fulfillment and joy. Deep inside I was refusing to settle for mediocrity. I looked for inspirations and studied the masters; I pushed myself out of a comfort zone and dared greatly.

I consciously designed and handcrafted the life I live today, and it is full of worldly travel and realized passions. I have friends in many countries. My marriage is blissful. I am blessed with the ability to help people and be a catalyst for amazing transformations in their lives, and I absolutely love what I do.

None of what I have was handed to me on a silver platter—neither my relationship nor my lifestyle. Moreover, a blissful life cannot be given to you. No matter what your starting place, creating joyful experiences and success is solely your choice. Being born into fortune is not always a blessing and has its own challenges. People often equate wealth with happiness, but the two are completely unrelated. My husband and I are not rich in the traditional sense, but the happiness we share is our main prosperity.

I invite you to embark on a journey to discovering true love. When you learn to ride the waves of raging seas and gracefully face ghastly winds, your heart will open up to infinite sunshine, and your eyes will see beauty that words cannot describe. May your *spirit* be your guide!

The Journey to
Happily Ever After

Like most people, I dreamed of sharing my life with someone special. My heart yearned for a deep connection to another soul and for happiness. I imagined feeling adored and cherished; I wanted to have fun, be creative, and feel inspired to surprise and delight my mate. I dreamed of friendship, romance, adventure, and true love—all with the *one*.

For many years, however, those dreams seemed unattainable. One after another, my relationships fell apart, or I kept dating the wrong people. I started to doubt if true, courageous, openhearted love and the *one* even existed. It seemed an overwhelmingly difficult task to find the right partner and to maintain a relationship that would not run out of steam. Was I too bold to expect that somebody would accept and love me for who I was and that this person would share my values, aspirations, and many of my interests? I was scared that even if I were to find the right mate, I might get bored with him, or he would come to want someone else.

Do people ever play "all in" in the mating game, I wondered, or did that phenomenon only exist in chick-flick movies and romantic novels? If I fell in love, could I trust myself not to be blinded by temporary attraction and miss warning signs in my partner? What if I opened my heart and got hurt? Perhaps it's simply easier to have fun and avoid dealing with commitment and drama altogether. Maybe it's worth settling for calculated compatibility and comfort. Often, people feel lonelier in relationships than when they were single.

These concerns kept rising in my mind, pushing me to lower my expectations and go after something more "reasonable." Friends and family added pressure by nagging, "What are you waiting for?" So I gave in and tried. First I had a marriage of convenience; then "love in a cottage;"[1] then a "no strings attached" agreement; and a multitude of dating scenarios in between. In these attempts to settle for less than I really wanted, I was denying a part of myself. These socially-inspired arrangements were doomed. I was never going to be happy without fully living my dreams.

If any of this applies to you, then this book will lend you a helping hand. I eventually learned to listen to my inner voice as a guide. I went on a journey looking for timeless treasures and found more than I ever expected to. Now my reality by far outweighs the dreams I once had, even though my husband does not own an Aston Martin (yet).

When you are in love, you are not only in love with a particular person; you are in love with life itself and every part of it. I want *you* to be in love and to embrace yourself and life fully. This book is a key that will open your heart, which has all the maps and strategies you will ever need to find your treasures.

Somehow my husband and I have come to know and enjoy what most people are missing. Our ongoing co-creation is a heavenly partnership of passion and love. Descriptions and words alone are incapable of relating such an experience. Try to describe fireworks to someone who has never seen them; no explanation will come close to seeing them firsthand. I want you to experience your fireworks! This is why I wrote this book.

---

1   A love affair without sufficient means

Verifying
the Principles

I was wondering whether the formula that worked for our relationship
was unique to us or whether other people could successfully apply it. I
searched for couples whose relationships were truly extraordinary and
conducted thorough interviews with them. My extensive research confirmed
time and again that the principles our union was founded on are universal.

Many brilliant masters of life and relationships shared their wisdom and
personal stories for this book. In particular, you will learn from Mikki Willis
and Nadia Salamanca—California-based filmmakers and the founders of the
socially and environmentally conscious media company Elevate (www.elevate.
us). Nadia and Mikki have crossed a ten-year mark in their marriage without
having had a single fight. They advocate love without drama and graciously
share their insights. They are openhearted and genuine people. Together
they led missions to bring clean water to third-world countries, build homes
for the homeless, create schools in Africa, and deliver musical equipment
to children in postwar territories. Each one of them experienced a defining
moment in life, which triggered more profound understanding and inspired

them to direct their creativity and efforts toward uniting people and finding ways to help.

For Mikki the eye-opener was witnessing the collapse of the twin towers during the 9/11 attacks, from a neighboring high-rise. He volunteered to participate in the rescue mission and remained in the danger zone for three consecutive days in search of survivors. Facing death and tragedy evoked deep compassion in him and made him reconsider his values. As a result, Mikki's career and life took a new direction.

Adverse events had also pushed Nadia to shift her priorities in life, when her boyfriend of several years was murdered. Coping with the loss and regaining her balance led Nadia to new understandings and helped to reinforce her inner strength. The healing work she went through helped her build a solid foundation within. Consequently, now she is able to wear many hats, successfully and gracefully. Nadia is a loving wife and a devoted life partner, caring mother, and a sharp businesswoman. She is a co-creator of Elevate Film Festival, Elevate Foundation, Elevate Films, and of a new revolutionary platform PlayitFWD (www.playitfwd.com). This distribution system allows people to share the movies they liked with others for a small fee by simply sending an e-mail link to a pre-paid film that can be viewed online.

Another contributor is Peggy McColl—an internationally recognized expert in personal and professional development, entrepreneur, and a *New York Times* best-selling author of *Your Destiny Switch* (www.peggymccoll. com). Peggy and her husband, Denis, formed an exciting and fulfilling union in their forties. It was not the first marriage for either of them, and their relationship involved building a rapport with stepchildren and ex-spouses. However, their partnership is a vivid demonstration that harmony at home can be created regardless of how many elements need balancing.

Much wisdom and helpful tips were shared by Mali Apple and Joe Dunn— the authors of the award-winning book *The Soulmate Experience*. Joe and Mali are not married, but they have been together for over eight years, and their union is truly remarkable. They established a deep soulful connection even before they met in person. They found each other online, and in order to keep their communication pure and not allow physical appearance to get in the way, Mali and Joe didn't exchange pictures for a few weeks. Now they coach couples and individuals and pass on their insights. In addition, they host a rapidly growing Facebook community with tens of thousands of members.

Profound insights and practical tips also came from Dianne and Alan Collins who have co-created a fantastic marriage for over twenty-three years. Dianne is one of the thought leaders of our time, visionary, philosopher, and the author of *Do You Quantum Think?* Alan is a master QuantumThink coach and consultant (www.quantumthink.com). Together they conduct various personal and corporate programs designed to revolutionize an approach to thinking and produce substantial results.

Many other incredible people supported the *Best Thing Ever* project and shared their experiences and advice. The path has been paved for you.

I took a bumpy road on the way to my extraordinary marriage. I missed many turns, went on detours, and was trapped in dead ends. When I reached a smooth highway, I realized that the ride didn't have to be hard. If you get directions in advance and follow them, you will have a fun and adventurous journey. I've mapped out for you a scenic route, so you can savor every mile and take advantage of shortcuts.

It is Easier than You Think

"Do you remember where you came from before you
were here?" Amber Hartnell asked her two-and-a-half-
year-old son, Surama. He nodded and said, "Yes."
"Can you tell me what it was like?"
He flashed his knowing smile and clearly replied,
"The place where we share one heart."

"Love" is the most powerful word in any language. Love
appeals to our soul's deepest desires and subconsciously calls
us home—to our spiritual essence. Any divine, sublime, or
pleasurable experience is associated with love. Both our greatest joys and our
deepest pains are linked to love, or its absence. Through romantic love and
the most sacred of all relationships—the intimate partnership—we experience
unsurpassed fulfillment and the exhilarating feeling of being alive. The divine
privilege to consciously create new life also springs from the intimate union.

However, the sacred word "love" has been greatly abused by our society. It is often applied toward expressions that stem from fears and insecurities, or attempts to gain control over others. For example, being concerned for someone's well-being is not a communication of love, but of fear. Expecting another person to change is not love, but arrogance. And attempting to hold on to somebody or to compete for his or her attention is a sign of insecurity. One of the greatest high-performance coaches of our time, Anthony Robbins, explains that there are four types of love:

1. **Baby Love**—when we show affection and "love" only when our demands are satisfied, just like a spoiled kid who behaves nicely as long as others cater to him, but turns into a monster if they don't. This is the most primitive egocentric type. It is blackmail rather than love.

2. **Conditional Love or "Horse-trading"**—when "love" is given with an expectation of reciprocity. Consciously or subconsciously, we keep track of what we have given, and if the payoffs do not come, we get upset and withdraw our "love."

3. **Real Love**—when we offer our care and warmth as a pure manifestation of our souls' essence. We expect nothing in return, and the giving itself is gratifying.

4. **Spiritual Love**—when we love every living creature, including those who hurt us.

In my experience, the first two types are not love and should be addressed by their real name—*manipulations*. "Real love" and "spiritual love" are one and the same. The only difference is the outreach, which depends on our ability to feel connection with *all of life*. In truth, there is only one type of love: the one that shines from the purity of your heart and is given unequivocally.

Sincere relationships are simple. Complex theories, classifications, and therapeutic approaches are developed around dysfunctions. Real love is the easiest and most natural thing in the world because it is aligned with our core spiritual nature. When we get caught up in manipulations, we lose clarity. By lying to ourselves and to others, we stop following our intuition and end up making painful mistakes. I've lost touch with the truth in my heart many times. And so life seemed very hard, and relationships were complicated and stressful.

By contrast, when I met my husband, we were both openhearted and genuine. There were no games or doubts. This approach made our relationship flow easily; it is joyous, fun, and lighthearted. We got married in two months from the day we met. Today we are happier than ever before.

Truth be told, we were both ready. We had made our share of mistakes in the past and had done the work to figure out what we really wanted before we met. We both were available and self-sufficient. Neither of us was dating anyone or had emotional attachments, and we were independent—financially and otherwise. Of course, there were some challenges. We lived in different states. Aleksey lived in Arizona, where he had a job, a mortgage, his entire family, and friends; I lived in Los Angeles. Logically, it should have slowed us down. Instead, because we were driven by pure purpose and our hearts' sincere desire, and focused on what we wanted rather than how to get there, miracles happened. We were in love and felt blissful. Everything around us, including people and circumstances, turned into living magic. Aleksey's job moved to California with him. His boss granted him permission to work from home. Not only was he able to maintain uninterrupted employment after his move, but he also fulfilled his long-time dream of telecommuting. Within two days he had rented out his house. My roommate was already planning to move out, and Aleksey moved in the very next day. Every little detail of our moving in together worked out with remarkable ease and precision. The power of the Universe and *Love* in all its glory gracefully delivered the impossible.

To this day, serendipities and miracles are our daily experience, and we take pride in creating them. I call these especially romantic, fun, or exhilarating episodes "Magic Moments." At the end of each section of this book, I will share with you a Magic Moment from my experience with Aleksey or the stories kindly contributed by other successful couples. Usually romantic films or tales will end with the pair walking into the sunset on a beach or driving away together in a car, where the actual life of a happy duo is never portrayed. The audience is left unaware of whether they are still holding hands twenty years into their marriage. In order for you to create an extraordinary relationship, you have to have a good idea of what it would be like on daily basis. Therefore, I'd like to lift the veil of private lives of many successful couples and offer you a glimpse into their casual fairy tales.

Use these digressions from the main premise as inspiration, and imagine yourself in similar scenarios. This will activate your creative powers and will charge you with positive anticipation. If you can recall related instances from your own past, savor and cherish these memories and indulge in their every detail. I invite you to become an originator and collector of Magic Moments and to share them with others at www.BestThingEver.com. Wouldn't it be great to pass on to your children a book of Magic Moments, so that when the time comes for your descendants to create an enduring intimate union of their own, they will have a vivid example and a strong point of reference? Besides, accumulating pleasant experiences versus complaints is one sure way to become happier as an individual or as a couple, because you always receive more of what you focus on.

You deserve to bring your own fairy tale into reality, and it's much easier than you might think. It's certainly more natural than any tricks you might learn on how to *Make Him Commit and Think It's His Idea* or *How to Get Beautiful Women into Bed*. Such games are devious and are deadly for real love. Exploring your own inner essence will evoke your acceptance and deep appreciation, which will allow you to relax into unity with another human being and experience incomparable joy of true intimacy.

Magic Moment

Our feet dig deeply into the warm white sand of Flamingo Beach, as we walk along the water's edge. We have grown to love our daily ritual of walking and then swimming in the ocean right before sunset. A warm tropical breeze is carrying heavy clouds that quickly begin to darken the sky. It will rain; it is inevitable now. As heavy drops begin kissing the ground, we decide to go swimming. We will be soaking wet anyway. The ocean welcomes us like a cozy blanket, as it is warmer than the air and much warmer than the sky shower. We swim far out, while the raging storm continues to spew streams of water, thunder, and lightning. The sun begins setting, painting the sky with pink, orange, and purple strokes. It is surreally transcendent. As we are returning to shore, the red disc of the sun shining through the grey-blue haze majestically touches the ocean at the horizon. We are still about waist-deep in the crystal emerald water. Aleksey lifts me up into his arms and starts spinning me around and kissing me. We drink the rain off each other's skin, laughing, and appreciating life and love, the vastness of the sky above and the exquisiteness of our planet.

PART II

Your Relationship Purpose

Why Be in a Relationship?

Tears were rolling down my cheeks. For the past few hours, I had been crying on and off because I was terrified. Every time the big screens of the Los Angeles Convention Center showed the logs on fire, I panicked. These logs would become the coals that we were to walk over. On the stage, Tony Robbins was enthusiastically explaining that their temperature would be 2,000 degrees Fahrenheit. My decision to walk on the fire was firm. But I knew that unless I overcame the fear, I would end up in a hospital needing treatment for burns. My grit was unshakable. This time I wanted to step over to the other side. I was determined to move beyond the subconscious elusive fear that for so many years had been preventing me from achieving greater success. I had had enough of settling for less. Once and for all, I wanted to conquer whatever it was inside me that had been pulling the hand brake and effectively reasoning me out of taking that next step. If I could conquer my fear and walk on hot coals, this would mean that I could walk over any fear in the future.

Now it was time to go. Hundreds of barefoot people started marching outside. I procrastinated. My action partner—a lovely woman from Germany, named Petra—was waiting patiently for me. We were supposed to walk together and support each other; I could not let her down. So I took off my shoes and started walking toward the exit. As we joined the crowd, everybody around us seemed excited and ready. Everyone but me. I was still shaking and about to burst into tears again. As we progressed down the street, I saw the police cars with their emergency lights on. Clouds of smoke were rising in the air from the fenced parking lot. Somewhere nearby there must be an ambulance, I thought.

Soon the rumble of drums filled the space. They sounded deeply primal and resonated in my spirit. All of a sudden I started moving, hopping from one foot to the other, loosely waving my hands, performing some kind of a tribal dance. I needed to shake off my fear or do something to regain my inner freedom and composure. Amazingly, after a few minutes of this primal dancing, the muscle tension in my body subsided, and I felt elevated and confident. I was ready.

The crowd thickened as we approached the strips of hot coals. A few women passed by us on their way back. They said that walking on those coals was a crazy idea and there was no way in hell they were going to do it. Regardless, Petra and I kept moving forward. Secretly I was hoping that by the time we got there the coals would have cooled off a bit. But just as we were about to walk, the crew decided to add new red-hot smoky coals to the strip.

Petra went first and waited for me on the other side. There was no choice but for me to go, too. A trainer at the beginning of the strip checked my state for readiness and commanded me to go. As I marched on sizzling embers, I did not feel a thing. It seemed so easy that right after I was done screaming happily into Petra's ear (I still feel sorry about that), I started to doubt the fact that I had actually walked on fire. Funny thoughts, like maybe I was lucky not to get burned, or maybe the coals were not hot enough, or maybe I went too fast, started creeping into my head. I wanted to be absolutely sure that I had really done it and could replicate my accomplishment at any time. So despite Tony Robbins' instructions to go only once, Petra and I went again. This time

I got a few tiny burns, which were almost gone by the next day. But this was confirmation that the coals were indeed hot.

Firewalking is a metaphor for stepping over challenges and obstacles. I was overcoming the actual dread of burns and pain, but with that, I was declaring the power of my spirit over any fear or hardship. If I did not have very strong reasons to do it, I would've never been able to step beyond my paralyzing fright and walk on fire. Just wanting something was not good enough.

Most individuals say they want happy relationships, health, wealth, true friendships, and more. But relatively few experience those things, because the majority is not ready to take the steps necessary to accomplish their desires: whether it means being honest with themselves, exercising regularly, taking risks, or learning new things. People who achieve their ambitions have strong reasons that propel them forward. It is crucially important for you to understand clearly the reasons why you want to be in a lasting relationship; what is its purpose?

Gaining clarity on your "why" will help you:

1. **Clarify your relationship vision.** Once you know the purpose of your relationship, crafting a compelling vision will be a breeze. Your "why" will shape your universal aims and desires into defined objectives and will transform them into tangible experiences in the future.

2. **Inspire your personal growth.** A relationship will help you grow like nothing else. It prompts you to open up, and it requires grace and complete acceptance of another and yourself. To get ready for the relationship of your dreams, you may need to do some preliminary work, weeding out limiting beliefs or releasing ties to your ex-lovers. Your "why" will be a catalyst for your progress.

3. **Attract and recognize the right partner.** Understanding what kind of experience you want to have will help you define the characteristics of your future mate. You will know in your gut what it should feel like to be with the *one*, and this reference point will make recognizing her easy.

4. **Keep your relationship magical on a daily basis.** When you firmly know the outcomes you are after, maintaining a great partnership becomes easy and natural. This will simply require the alignment of your actions and words with the purpose of your relationship.

5. **See and celebrate your progress.** It is common to measure the success of a relationship in terms of the time a couple has been together. In my experience, a far more effective way of evaluating this is to see if an intimate relationship is serving its purpose. Is it a significant source of joy and fulfillment? Your powerful "why" will keep you on track and will prompt you to change course when necessary.

Find Your "Why"

he importance of a personal relationship is different for everyone. Some find their bliss in celibacy. Since you have picked up this book, I assume that an intimate partnership is important to you and that you deem it necessary for a vibrant and fulfilling life experience. What constitutes a "healthy" or "extraordinary" relationship is also unique for each person, and you will decide what it entails for you. For me it means the following:

- waking up joyous every morning next to the person I love
- expressing care, love, and tenderness toward each other always
- being playful and making each other laugh often
- admiring my partner and being proud of him
- having fun and embarking on adventures together
- feeling cherished and adored
- melting in his arms and loving his touch
- learning new things and growing together

- stimulating each other intellectually
- sharing responsibilities
- uniting our efforts
- uplifting each other
- dreaming together
- designing our life to fulfill our dreams
- being inspired to delight my mate

My own definition of an "extraordinary" relationship is that every moment we are together is a precious gift making me feel alive and happy.

The questions below are designed to extract from your subconscious mind the unique meaning you assign to intimacy and partnership in your life. Take the time to put your answers down in writing. You will have to imagine both scenarios: having an extraordinary and lasting union with the *one*, versus never fulfilling your dreams of a great personal relationship. Imagine yourself at a fork in the road. Before you decide which way to go, you have to know what awaits you at the end of each path. It is necessary to consider both outcomes so that you comprehend fully what is at stake.

Ready? Get situated in a secluded place, grab plenty of paper and a pen, make sure there are no distractions, and begin writing.

1. What will a passionate, devoted lover give you that you do not currently have?
2. If you had a fantastic personal relationship, how would your life be different?

3. What would it be like to live with the love of your life?
4. How will your great intimate relationship affect other aspects of your life: career, personal time, interests, hobbies, finances?
5. How will being happy in your personal life affect your health and mood?
6. Will you be fulfilled without a meaningful, intimate relationship?
7. What would living with the "good enough" person feel like?
8. Imagine living alone ten years from now. What would it be like?
9. What would living alone feel like in twenty years?
10. What would living alone feel like thirty years from now?
11. What life experiences will you never have if you do not create a passionate, lasting relationship?
12. How will you prepare your children for true intimacy if you fail to accomplish it in your personal life?

When you finish, take a look at your answers. Summarize them in one to three sentences to reflect what is most important to you and to answer the question, "What is the purpose of a great intimate relationship?" You might find it easier to have a buffer of time—usually overnight—between answering the questions and condensing them into your powerful "why" statement.

Below I will share my own answer to this question and the answers of wonderful people I interviewed, including my husband. However, I recommend you complete the above exercise before reading on, because mining for uninfluenced truth from your heart of hearts is invaluable. Uncovering your genuine reasons will give you tremendous confidence and inner strength.

This was my answer: "An intimate connection is the greatest source of fulfillment and fun. At the same time, it poses an ongoing challenge to look for the truth in my heart and to see the reality behind the curtains of illusion."

Aleksey: "A great intimate relationship inspires me to grow spiritually. I want my lover and me to become much more than just two people, to become a sacred, divine and life-giving entity. I want to pave the way for our children to come into this world. Leading by example is the best way to inspire our children to live from the heart, be true to themselves, and, when the time comes, to create great intimate relationships of their own."

Here is what Peggy McColl—a best-selling author and a happily married woman—shared about her union with her husband, Denis: "When you are in a healthy relationship, it brings out the best of who you are and just makes everything so much more worthwhile. Having Denny in my life has enhanced my career, my financial situation, my health, and my self-image... just everything. I feel better in every way!"

When asked about the purpose of their relationship, Dianne Collins—a lifetime scholar and intellectual—said, "The purpose of a relationship is multidimensional. Just like your connection happens on different levels... For me, one of the purposes is to reach self-realization; some people say "God-realization"—reaching the highest enlightened state through a relationship." Dianne's husband and business partner, Alan, added: "If people have done their work in creating a purpose for their relationship, that in and of itself will pull them through whatever is going on in the circumstantial world of the moment."

Another enlightening answer came from Mali Apple and Joe Dunn—award-winning authors and relationship coaches: "The purpose of a relationship is to have somebody to share the magic of life with. It's much more rewarding than just going out there and doing it by yourself. It sort of doubles...or triples. It's like a partner in exploration."

Amber Hartnell[2], the star of the award-winning documentary *Orgasmic Birth*, a modern dancer, and pioneer of conscious living offered these wise words: "Every relationship is like walking into a room full of mirrors, where we can see different angles of ourselves to learn more deeply about who we are and how we function, what our gifts are, and what we enjoy and what we are challenged by. So, it's really experience and learning."

---

2   For more information about Amber go to www.embodiedresonance.com

Is There a
Soul Mate for Me?

When I was about eleven years old, I watched my very first soap opera. The main heroine met the man of her dreams, but soon after that, he tragically died. About twenty episodes later, she met someone else and fell in love again. This was shocking to my childish idealism. How could she be with another person? Isn't there only one perfect mate for each of us? Don't you meet your prince, fall in love with him, and live happily ever after?

I grew up understanding that we are not limited to a sole path of happiness, and our lives can take different turns and be joyously shared with more than one partner. It was liberating to realize that we are not bound to a single person for contentment and a blissful life. However, the question then becomes, if we have no pre-determined mate, what makes someone the *right* partner or the *one*?

Simply put, it is a mate with whom you can fulfill the purpose of your relationship. Whether a reason behind your romantic union is to experience fun and adventure, or lust and passion, or to feel secure and gain financial benefits, or to have children, the right partner is someone who can help you accomplish your goals. When you yearn for a multidimensional experience—a genuine and soulful connection on every level—physical, spiritual, emotional, and intellectual—the definition of the *love of your life* also becomes multifaceted.

In this case, the *one* is a chosen partner with whom you can craft a delightful and lasting relationship and create a truly wonderful and exciting life. Such a romantic union will enrich the lives of both of you in every single way. Your hearts will open to each other, and your aims, goals, and values will be in alignment. You will evoke the best in one another and become a mutual source of inspiration and encouragement. Each of you will feel more empowered and shine your brightest, reach for new heights and have more clarity than ever before. Loving your mate will feel like you are expanding. Your communication will be seamless, and your attraction will be very strong.

When your mutual love and deep appreciation grow, the two of you will frequently feel as one, as if your very souls intertwine and saturate each other. This kind of kinship is often called "soul mates," because your affinity is much more profound than similar interests and sexual chemistry. The *one* for you is the mirror of who you are. In order to recognize him, you have to see yourself clearly, feel your core, or your eternal essence, know your power, and keep your heart open to love.

Becoming the authentic—and thus best—version of yourself is all the work you'll ever have to do for your relationship. The *Life-giving Creative Source* of the Universe will take care of the rest, including attracting the mate of your dreams. And yes, there is a person, perhaps more than one, who is waiting to become your blissful co-creator of whatever experiences you desire.

> *Your task is not to seek for love, but merely to seek and find all the barriers within yourself that you have built against it.*
> —*A Course in Miracles* by Helen Schucman
> and William Thetford

Noteworthy

Every intimate partner you've ever had was a perfect match for you *in that time*. This is a bold statement, I know. What if a mate was violent, or abusive, or unfaithful—how could he have been perfect for you? Your lover and the dynamics of your relationship always reflect your perspectives on yourself, on others, and intimacy in general. A relationship magnifies each insecurity, concern, or anxiety you hold. If there is a fear of loneliness, or low self-esteem, we try to compensate the inner void with poor choices. This is when we settle for less or tell ourselves stories that justify someone treating us disrespectfully or negligently.

Nonetheless, these are learning experiences, which are almost inevitable for all of us. That is because in childhood and adolescence we were teased and called names by our peers; we were criticized by our parents and teachers; and we allowed the disapproval of others to imprint on our self-image. Initial heartbreaks offer valuable lessons that are supposed to prompt us to cultivate self-respect and confidence. Until we draw empowering conclusions and adjust our course, life will keep presenting its challenges. Through trial and error of our early relationships, we get to know ourselves better and define more clearly what we want. Once we decide that we deserve better, we move on, and usually things get better, unless we still cling to some rotten convictions about ourselves or others.

When you are authentic and honor yourself, you will hardly tolerate a mate who discourages you. And if you are poised and centered, you will never be attracted to an abusive partner in the first place. Your relationship will always match your inner state and your outlook on life. This is why in the following chapters we will break through the limits of conventional thinking, and I will introduce you to new possibilities for love and relationships. Also, you will start developing the necessary disposition to creating an extraordinary romance of your own.

Magic Moment

Kari Glinsky and Collin Hughes have been together for over ten years. Their mutual affection and care only grew and strengthened with time. Below is one of the stories from their everyday life.

"It was a Sunday morning. I was pleasantly sleeping in our cozy and comfortable bed. Collin's gentle and tender kisses woke me up. He looked at me so affectionately as if I were the most treasured being on the planet. My heart overflowed with joy, and I smiled. Then he gave me a card he'd made for me. Collin got up early to prepare this wonderful gift, which was not privy to any holiday or special occasion. He painted a picture of our much-loved house bunny named Moomin on the front and wrote me a note inside. Once again, I felt loved, adored, and blessed to have such an amazing man as my husband."

moomin-bunny
Collin Hughes 2.10.13

Feb. 10th 2013.
Kari
Baby, let there be no
context or reason for this
note, none whatsoever.
Just know that I love
you so much, so I made
this for you.
There are no words to
describe it. I have no way
to express it. You keep me
like a little kid all the time
so happy and excited. I
LOVE you so much. Collin

PART III

What Leads You Astray

Step Beyond Constraints

*What is popular is not always right,
and what is right is not always popular.*
—Howard Cosell, American broadcasting legend

We grow up absorbing and assimilating cultural beliefs and common sayings. After we hear something enough times, we adopt that belief and then it guides our thoughts and actions. Unfortunately, many common myths about relationships are products of failed unions. When you accept them as your truth, these misconceptions create major limitations on your life. You set boundaries on possibilities and lower your standards. Such beliefs become major obstacles on your way to a fulfilling partnership.

Media and most of casual conversations thrive on drama, problems, people's shortcomings, and mistreatments of each other. The subject of relationships is the juiciest source of gossip, scandals, and other pain-generating discussions. Unless you are a rare exception, you have been subjected to this stream of ill-natured information about relationships since early childhood. Even if your parents had a great marriage, you witnessed adults talking about friends, neighbors, or relatives going through traumatic personal experiences. Television and movies portrayed emotionally charged breakups, and magazine covers screamed of celebrity cheaters. Your self-preservation instincts linked caution and fear to the idea of intimacy, and your own first heartbreak came as solid proof of your concerns. For some people this leads to avoiding intimacy altogether.

In order to welcome a blissful relationship into your life, you have to believe that it is possible and to disassociate from the pains of the past. That is because *you don't get what you want—you get what you think is possible.* Wherever you set the reality limits for yourself is how far your experience can reach. It's like installing a speed governor on a vehicle—no matter how hard you push on the gas pedal, the car will not go any faster than the governor's restriction. For instance, if you want to create a lasting marriage, but believe that the "honeymoon stage" does not last forever, then the extent of your blissful days will be constrained by your own perceptions. Should you think that "all the good ones are taken," you will constantly be attracted to people who are unavailable.

This is why aligning your wishes with your beliefs and resolving any inner conflicts is fundamental. Breaking free from old anxieties requires disassociating from misleading conventions and adapting new perspectives. Let's take a look at the ten most dangerous common myths. They are the ultimate formulae for disappointment, frustration, arguments, and resentment. I urge you to understand and assess your own misbeliefs and embrace a more empowering outlook. To help you do that, an example of an Empowering Statement is offered at the end of each chapter.

Myth 1

A Relationship Is Hard Work

We do not perceive an artist's inspired creation of a masterpiece to be "hard work." Even if this process takes months or years, we understand that she draws pleasure from the creative act. We refer to relationships as "hard work" when we talk about doing something unwanted or against our will. It implies cautious or even unnatural behavior, calculating steps, making an effort, sacrificing, putting up with annoying things, etc.

In a happy union your lover accepts you fully and evokes your best from you. In return, you appreciate and completely embrace your mate, inspiring the best in her. Both of you express your feelings openly, relying on each other for support and understanding, and no one is walking on eggshells. When an intimate partnership feels like "hard work," it is a sign of trouble.

For my husband and me, our relationship is the easiest and most natural thing. I also asked blissful couples if the common perception of "working" for a relationship rang true for them, and every pair I interviewed strongly disagreed.

Joe Dunn and Mali Apple first laughed at the question. Then Joe said, "Oh, no. Not at all! It never felt like our relationship has been hard work. I think a great relationship takes focus and intention, but it never feels like work at all. It feels like fun!" Then Mali chimed in: "Because you are not doing something you don't want to do..."

Peggy McColl said, "I don't think it's hard work at all. If you've got your values in alignment, I don't think it should be hard work; it should be fun! I think people make things far more complicated than they need to be."

In fact, my question often evoked utter surprise from people as to why I would ask something so odd. This is because in the world of happy couples their union is a sanctuary—delightful and effortless. A sincere relationship is akin to singing in unison or playing music together—a pleasurable and enthused exploration of new harmonies and sounds. It is an inspired and ongoing process that requires tools and skills and calls for devoted participation of both partners. Yet, it never becomes a burden or a requirement. Rather it serves as the greatest source of satisfaction, excitement, and happiness in one's life. An intimate union is a joyful co-creation that makes life easier because you have someone to count on, to provide support when necessary, and to share responsibilities.

> *Empowering Statement:* An intimate relationship is fun! It is a powerful catalyst to fulfillment, joy, and personal growth.

Myth 2

It's Give and Take

The social concept of fairness is very pronounced in our culture. Studies reveal that we are guided by this subjective principle. During experiments conducted by behavioral economists, participants were willing to turn down free money if they felt that the amount of money they were offered was unfair. The popular opinion that a relationship is "give and take" is related to this prevalent principle of fairness. "You scratch my back and I'll scratch yours" sounds like a fair statement, doesn't it? In this scenario, couples subconsciously keep track of their "investments"

SIGN HERE... OKAY... AND IT SAYS I'M TO WAIT HERE FOR A RECIPROCAL PACKAGE. INDEFINITELY.

in the relationship and look for ways to cash out. This is a perfect recipe for misery and dissatisfaction.

"Fair" implies an exchange between two separate entities. A romantic union, on the other hand, is *one entity*. Therefore, the elements within it—the partners—should contribute *all they've got* to the benefit of the whole.

Joe Dunn shared wise words: "We do not come into a relationship fifty-fifty at everything. In some cases I am better than Mali; in a lot of cases she is better than I am. We look for those places where we can contribute more of our gift or ability, so we contribute more in those areas. And we don't say, 'So, I gave fifty percent and you have to give the other fifty percent.' That's crazy! It doesn't work that way, and it will never work that way. You just breed resentment. I think a lot of people do this, 'Well, I did this, so you have to do that, it makes it even and balanced.' No! How about, I give a hundred percent what I am great at doing and you give a hundred percent at what you are great at doing, and we will all be happy."

A genuine relationship is rooted in a sincere desire to give. If you ever truly loved anyone or anything, you would know that there is really no measure on how much you give. Love fills up your entire being and starts overflowing, and your giving is a natural outcome of this brimming. You can never give too much, because no matter how much you have already contributed, you are still inspired to do more. Just like the sun cannot not shine and give warmth, you cannot not give your love and care to another. This is who you are and how you express yourself. A sincere partner who deeply cares for you will do the same.

The word "take" does not even apply to a great relationship. "Receiving" and "appreciation" are much more suitable. The need to *take* comes from the feelings of scarcity and lack. Resulting demands and expectations are incompatible with true love, because they are rooted in fear. We withdraw our love only because we fear being hurt. Yet, nothing hurts us more than denying our own essence.

> *Empowering Statement:* An intimate relationship liberates my heart to a free flow of love.

Myth 3

Relationships Require Sacrifice

Self-sacrifice, we drool, is the ultimate virtue. Let's stop and think for a moment. Is sacrifice a virtue? Can a man sacrifice his integrity? His honor? His freedom? His ideal? His convictions? The honesty of his feeling? The independence of his thought? But these are a man's supreme possessions. Anything he gives up for them is not a sacrifice but an easy bargain. They, however, are above sacrificing to any cause or consideration whatsoever. Should we not, then, stop preaching dangerous and vicious nonsense? Self-sacrifice? But it is precisely the self that cannot and must not be sacrificed. It is the unsacrificed self that we must respect in man above all.
—Ayn Rand, *The Fountainhead*

The noble-sounding idea of sacrifice is in fact counterproductive. It forces a person to make choices unwillingly for the sake of a relationship or to please his partner. This approach always leaves a residue of dissatisfaction and regret for the loss of potential. Later it translates into subtle or openly voiced reproaches like "I moved for you," "I gave up my hobbies and friends for you," "I left my career to take care of children," etc.

Self-sacrifice takes the corrupt approach of "I do this for you, so you can do something for me"—namely "give and take"—and puts a noble cover over it that says, "I don't want anything in return; I will just sacrifice for you, because I love you." Yet, it creates an even worse moral dependency, where the receiver of a sacrifice becomes almost guilty and either has to sacrifice in return, or expressly demonstrate gratitude forever.

Sacrifice is often used as a hypocritical form of manipulation, designed to instill obligation in another. Have you ever received a favor from someone who later reminded you repeatedly of what he or she has done for you? How did it make you feel? Did you wish at times that you did not ask for that favor at all?

In addition, sacrifice is not about what you do or don't do for another, but rather your attitude toward your own choices. By sacrificing you take the position of a victim to the forces greater than you, where you "have to" or "must" perform a certain action. This is actually never true, even if it often seems otherwise, because there is always an agenda or purpose behind any decision you make, whether you consciously acknowledge it or not.

For instance, nursing a baby requires significant exertion from any mother. Yet, some mothers will treat their children as gifts of God, affectionately taking care of them and offering unconditional love. They will say, "Yes, raising children was hard, but so worth it!" Others, however, will present a moral "bill" to their grown kids reminding them of sleepless nights, intense and painful labors, and other "sacrifices" they had to make, thereby pulling a guilt trip, and coercing their offspring into a certain behavior. These demands can range from getting an impressive degree to marrying a respected person, or adopting prestigious interests in order to make the mother proud. In the first case, a mother realizes that it was her choice to have a baby and feels appreciative for being able to create a new life and experience motherhood. In the second situation, the mother turns parenting into a favor to her child and presents a list of expectations in return.

The obligatory phrases that begin with "I have to," "I must," or "I should" are often followed by the list of unwanted consequences that will surface otherwise. Always, however, there is also a list of desirable outcomes of any action. Try to substitute these requisite expressions with "I choose to, because." For example, rather than saying "I have to work, because I've got bills to pay," say "I choose to work, because it allows me to pay my bills, afford things, and to be of value to others."

Changing your perspective from sacrifice to a deliberate choice will transform your self-perception from a dutiful casualty to life's tough circumstances into a powerful human being who is in charge and proud of her contributions. Your new attitude will inevitably affect your state of affairs, which will start improving before your very eyes. It will also free your loved ones from indebtedness to you.

It is common to think that when you love someone, the beloved is the main beneficiary. In truth, the main recipient of your blessings is you. That is because by loving another you align with your real essence, and you get to express your core nature. It allows you to become the ultimate embodiment of the divine. In this sense love does not require any reciprocity. Consequently, unrequited love is socially constructed nonsense. Sexual desire can be unreturned, or obsession can be one-sided; real love, on the other hand, is fulfilling in and of itself. It is actually irresistible.

Real intimacy is based on honesty. If you deeply care for your beloved, you would never want her to "sacrifice" for you or do something that makes her uncomfortable. You will do everything to promote her well-being. A lover who cherishes you will never ask you to disadvantage yourself for her sake.

On the other hand, you may *want* to undergo some inconvenience, because the joy of seeing your partner happy or pleased outweighs your potential discomfort. For instance, seeing a movie that excites your mate but does not interest you, or rubbing his shoulders when you are tired. However, this is not sacrifice. It is a conscious choice from which you draw pleasure—the pleasure of doing something for another, the joy of giving. It is in caring for one another that we can express our love and tenderness. Unless you learn to draw pleasure from your contributions and from the things you do for your partner, you will always feel dissatisfied, undervalued, and unappreciated.

At work, if you dislike what you do, no matter how much money you make or how much recognition you receive, going to the office every day will be "hard" and feel like a sacrifice of your time, your natural talents, and your life. Conversely, if you love what you do, your efforts will be joyous. However, even the best job on the planet involves some tasks that are not pleasant and may require dealing with difficult people. Certainly, there will be occasional problems and complications. Yet, those challenges will seem minor and insignificant when you perform a labor of love. The same is true for your personal life. If your relationship is great, inconveniences or glitches appear trivial in comparison to the happiness you feel in your union.

Shortly after my husband and I met, I told him, "I do not want you to do anything for me, ever. Anything you do that pleases me, I want you to do from the sheer desire of your heart and only because it brings joy to *you*." It's not that I don't want his help with household chores or that he shouldn't give me flowers. To the contrary, I welcome and appreciate his every input. However, we both give sincerely, without keeping track and expecting reciprocity. This approach is conducive to being inspired to do something for another versus being obligated. It keeps both of us in a free and delightful flow instead of being on duty as a wife or a husband.

Empowering Statement: I love seeing my partner happy, and this often inspires me to go an extra mile.

Myth 4

My Mate Should Make Me Happy, and I Should Make My Mate Happy

While intimate partners are the greatest catalysts of joy for each other, happiness is the inner work of your spirit. If your contentment depends on outside factors, including people and circumstances, you are like a ship without a captain, in raging waters—out of control and in great danger. Any gust can rip your sail, and any wave can send you to the bottom. You must be in charge of your well-being and courageously navigate your life. Your partner—no matter how skilled, smart, or dedicated—cannot effectively sail your boat and his own simultaneously. No one can handle the unbearable responsibility of making you happy. Neither should you be in charge of your partner's happiness since it is out of your control.

Think about the concept of making someone happy. Is it even possible? Have you known someone in grief or depression? What could you do to make that person happy? If you tried hard enough and dedicated enough time and effort, you could help to distract her from troublesome thoughts and inspire temporary relief. To sustain the effect you would have to forsake your own life in continuous attempts to make that person content. Would you be fulfilled in this scenario and for how long? Won't you eventually start resenting this person and blame her for the sacrifices you had to make? This example is rather extreme. However, too many people jump through hoops to make their partner happy. This effort feels unnatural and one-sided. Inevitably, contempt starts growing toward the very person whose fulfillment was so important in the first place.

Happiness can be shared or inspired, but it cannot be induced. It comes from within, and it is up to each of us, individually, to choose to be happy. We will cover this subject in more detail in Part V, when we talk about finding your balance.

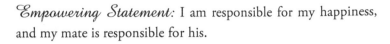

Empowering Statement: I am responsible for my happiness, and my mate is responsible for his.

Myth 5

A Relationship
Should Have a Timeline

I laugh out loud, as I glance through endless articles about who is supposed to say "I love you" first—the man or the woman—when is it okay to have sex, or to move in together, or introduce your partner to your family. The media go on and on: calculating the timing, the dangers of making a mistake, and possible recovery strategies. Should couples live together before getting married? How long should you date before the proposal? These nonsense discussions feed on the fear and insecurity in a relationship.

If you are afraid to be rejected, judged, or repelled by your lover, how are you planning to spend years of your life together? You can pretend and be cautious only for a short period of time. Eventually you will be tired of playing games and want to say what's on your mind and what you really feel like. A classic case of this is when people say, "It all was great before we got married, and then all hell broke loose."

The beauty of a healthy relationship lies in partners' full acceptance of each other, which allows both to be authentic and relaxed. It means trusting your mate to be kind and respectful of you, relying on his genuineness and the purity of his intent toward you. When your union is driven by sincere feelings, a purpose in your heart, and a powerful "why," these common confusions become irrelevant. My relationship with my husband developed entirely out of convention and broke every rule in existence. He told me that he was in love with me on the day we met, and after only two weeks he proposed, without a ring. I chose my own ring and wanted it to be an engagement and wedding ring all in one, and it was custom-made almost a year after our wedding.

Observers might have called us crazy, and then after our union proved to be successful—lucky. From the moment we met, both of us were honest with each other, so there was no need to calculate the next step strategically. We followed the natural progression and did what felt right in the moment. There is no "one size fits all" formula to follow. Every relationship is unique. People have different values, belief systems, and traditions they grew up with. You should care to know what is important to your beloved and also be expressive in telling him about your desires and goals. At the same time, following your heart is the best guidance available to you. And an open line of communication with your lover is the only preventive measure to avoid misunderstanding and confusion.

Empowering Statement: My relationship will unfold blissfully and organically, if I listen to my mind, trust my heart, and take inspired action.

Myth 6

Passion Inevitably Wanes

any people think that passion and excitement are only part of a relationship's initial stages. This keeps them from making a commitment, or motivates them to seek a new affair every time they become familiar with their existing partner. While there is no doubt that the quality of your passion for each other will transform, in a great partnership it becomes more profound and conscious, instead of hormone-driven.

A healthy relationship feels *alive*, which is impossible if passion is dead. Sexuality bonds partners on all levels: body, mind, and spirit. Feelings of oneness and deep connection are experienced through sexuality and develop over time. In order to understand why and how passion can intensify and grow, the fundamental approach to intimacy should be reconsidered.

Making love is different from having sex. When two bodies engage for the purpose of satisfying their instinctive needs, it is sex. Lovemaking is an emotional, spiritual, and physical expression of mutual love and devotion. During sex you only feel your body's sensations. When making love, in addition to your own pleasurable experience, you feel the ecstasy of your lover.

51

True magic in intimacy takes time. It is a sacred ritual and a manifestation of unity. It requires true care, trust, and knowing your partner very well to safely enter a new territory. Lovemaking is an infinite dimension that can never be fully explored.

When sexual desire declines and the intimate bond weakens, it is one of the first warning signs of a relationship problem. Dullness is a product of sameness. Routine and boredom are killers of passion. Variety, however, is not enough of a solution. Understanding the dynamics of masculine and feminine forces and the ability to consciously direct them is required.

For generations women fought for equality with men proving their capacity to succeed professionally, handle business affairs, and take powerful leadership positions. Many men were developing their sensitivity and gentleness, cultivating thoughtfulness and respect. While these developments were beneficial for social aspects of our lives, they negatively affected our intimate affairs. Sexual arousal, which is the foundation for creation of new life, thrives on the polarity of forces—yin and yang, or masculine and feminine. Equality does not spark mutual magnetism; in fact, similar charges repel each other. For mutual attraction, contrasting aspects of each quality should be present. If one of the partners is forceful, another should be submissive, if one is soft, another should be tough, etc. This is why proper girls often end up with bad guys, and good boys become henpecked.

Therefore, when an independent woman tries to remain in control when romantically interacting with men, she will either attract "nice" guys whom she will disrespect and will be dissatisfied with, or she will get into a power struggle with a more masculine man, which will lead to constant fights and a likely breakup. Respectively, a man who asks a woman "May I kiss you?" instead of simply embracing and kissing her when the moment feels right, is likely to end up with a bossy woman or to remain single for a long time by concluding that women want jerks. The solution is in identifying your core essence and magnifying it during intimate encounters.

For example, a bright, successful and powerful, yet feminine, woman would likely yearn for a man who is stronger than she is. In order to evoke masculine power in a man, she should release her own aggressive forces, become a soft and nourishing siren, open to vulnerability and let her man rule the love game. The same is true for a congenial and caring, but masculine, man who is hoping to find an affectionate and attentive woman. He should get a hold of his decisiveness and determination and claim his woman's heart and conquer her body through love. The roles can interchange, but when you pick a part you like to play, your partner has to play the opposite.

When living together and sharing responsibilities, it is easy to smooth the edges of masculine and feminine energies that were vividly pronounced during courtship. That is why it is important to learn to consciously evoke your predominant sensual nature and consequently arouse your partner, when intimate interaction is desired.

However, this subject is very broad and deserves its own book. My next work will cover it in depth. If you'd like to learn more about masculine and feminine dynamics and sexuality in the meantime, I recommend reading books by David Deida.

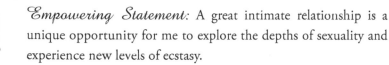

Empowering Statement: A great intimate relationship is a unique opportunity for me to explore the depths of sexuality and experience new levels of ecstasy.

Myth 7

You Can't
Have It All

"You should be realistic," "Don't set your standards too high," and my favorite, "You can't have it all" are all thoughtful concerns that supposedly protect you from potential disappointments. These are the same voices that call any enterprising new idea or endeavor impossible, and they come from people who settled for mediocrity by burying their own zest for life. Instead of encouraging you to reach for new heights, they would much rather see you play it comfortably safe because your achievements would remind them of their own shortcomings.

Your own insecurities, discouragements, and pains of past relationships may call

GOOD CONVERSATION WITH BAD SEX, OR GOOD SEX WITH BAD CONVERSATION? HAPPY ENDINGS NO LONGER AMUSE ME.

for self-preservation and trigger similar thoughts. Some people even "marry down" in order to make sure they are the superstar in a relationship, hoping that their spouse will try to hold on to them at all costs. In their mind, this protects them from infidelity and rejection. Obviously, this is not how healthy and lasting unions are formed.

Extraordinary relationships defy mediocre standards. I want to assure you that you can get anything and everything that is really important to you in your partner. The key is to focus on your genuine desires, disregarding what anyone else thinks or what is considered prestigious.

Some years into our marriage, I was going through old paperwork and found a journal where I described my future mate, which was long before I had met Aleksey. It was astounding how much my husband matched the description. Nonetheless, there were discrepancies. I asked for ocean-blue eyes so deep that I would want to drown in them, and Aleksey has green eyes—the most beautiful eyes I have ever seen. There were many silly things I wrote down, which I did not get. But who cares? Everything that was really important to me I received, including those things I did not realize were essential and did not include in my request.

What does it tell you? Dream big! Focus on the truth in your heart, and trust the wisdom of loving Infinite Intelligence or God to cater to your heart's deepest desires and to bring about what's best for you. We will talk about this in detail in the next section, where I will help you develop your relationship vision.

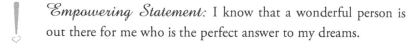

Empowering Statement: I know that a wonderful person is out there for me who is the perfect answer to my dreams.

Myth 8

My Partner Will Complete Me

We all yearn for a deep connection with others. Our intertwined nature calls us to the sacred home of oneness, which we often experience through intimacy. It gives us the feeling of wholeness, and the lover becomes a catalyst to this experience. So no wonder lovers associate each other with a sense of completeness. However, it is important to understand that the feeling of wholeness comes from within and should be cultivated before you meet the right person.

The idea of your partner completing you implies that you are incomplete. It introduces neediness and lack of self-sustainability into the equation. It burdens your lover with the responsibility to fill in the gaps and to keep you content. In turn, that creates the feeling of obligation and unnecessary pressure.

Has anyone ever told you they cannot live without you? If so, were you flattered or disturbed? I say you should be concerned. I was in a relationship once where my boyfriend repeatedly spoke words of love, but almost threatened to commit suicide at the thought of us parting ways. Of course he survived our breakup and even thrives without me. It was a sign of desperation, not love. Such behavior is a form of blackmail or subconscious manipulation often used by insecure individuals to compel you to behave in a way that enhances their feeling of certainty. Needy people are pitied and treated leniently, but not respected. Dignity is vital in a healthy relationship. It comes from confidence, independence, and the ability to stand on your own.

Two broken pieces do not make a whole. Imagine two birds, each one with an injured wing. One has the left wing damaged, the other, the right. If these birds got together as a couple, could they complete each other and fly? No. Even if only one of the birds had a broken wing, they wouldn't soar together in the sky. You have to take care of yourself and make sure you can fly and find a partner who can join you. Do not wait for anyone to gift you wings, for you were born with them. Spread them and explore the depths of the sky even before your mate comes along.

Also, don't try to persuade anyone to fly with you or attempt to fix his or her seeming inability to rise high. You won't help them and will remain on the ground yourself. The beauty of your flight will inspire others to glide in the air, and someone brave will join you in reaching for the stars.

> *Empowering Statement:* I have to get in touch with my own strength within so that my intimate partner and I can create a powerful union.

Myth 9

I Have to Understand the Opposite Gender

fairly recent idea that "men are from Mars, and women are from Venus" offers a promising insight into the mysterious world of the opposite sex. We get seduced by the potential of "thinking like a man" or "understanding women," believing that it will finally spell out the rules of the mating game and will allow us to get ahead of competitors. Trying to solve the puzzle of the opposite gender's world keeps our minds entertained and busy. Unfortunately, it renders mediocre and short-lived results.

Recognizing that there are gender differences is important, and knowing what they are is very useful. However, you can never fully comprehend how the opposite sex thinks or operates. That's simply because you're wired differently.

Every moment, you are subconsciously reading hundreds of subtle signals coming from your partner, ranging from body language to the tone of voice. By trying to process these indicators logically, you clutter the clarity of your intuition and pigeonhole your mate and her behavior. Focusing on acting in a particular way will diminish the authenticity of your relationship. You will over-think and overanalyze things. Your responses will be wiredrawn and unoriginal, and your timing will be off.

Instead, learn to *feel* your partner. It means focusing your undivided attention on your beloved and feeling her with your own heart. You will tune in to your mate and will *know* her. This way you will eliminate all guessing games. When you are in sync with each other, your very soul will give you all the answers you need. The perfect words and timely actions will be inspired. Your communication will be smooth and easy. In the following chapters, you will receive practical tools to help you hone this vital skill.

> *Empowering Statement:* I can never fully understand my partner, but I can open my heart to him, accept and embrace him completely and appreciate every bit of who he is.

Myth 10

Marriage Kills Romance

There is no doubt that marriage or living together significantly differs from dating. There are errands, routines, and responsibilities. There are moods, problems, and an occasional sickness. There is less mystery and more familiarity. At the same time, in a great committed relationship, you know each other's preferences and habits, you've developed inside jokes and sexual innuendos, and you've learned to trust and appreciate each other more than ever before. You have grown roots into each other's hearts and discovered new levels of depth you did not know were possible.

Marriage and commitment are supposed to signify the exquisiteness of the connection between the mates and the depth of their love for each other. Unfortunately, for many people it means entering into a binding agreement with obligatory terms applicable to both parties—for example, "tying the knot" on one's neck and suffocating him with marital duties and rules. Possessiveness, expectations, and the attitude of entitlement are sure killers of affection, desire, tenderness, and fun.

The creative approach to intimacy sparks from freedom of expression. Flirtation, playfulness, and arousal sprout from self-confidence and thrive in the atmosphere of approval and trust. When curiosity and fantasies are encouraged, the opportunities for new experiences are endless. Obviously, both lovers should be eager initiators and grateful recipients of new ideas and open-minded explorers of untapped terrains.

Romance, like passion, is a matter of choice. A creative mind can romance every moment. You can start dancing in your kitchen while singing a tune, or start a pillow fight in the morning; you can sneak flowers into your wife's closet, or take your husband to a surprise picnic. Romance is ruined not by marriage, but by taking life too seriously. The secret to never-ending romance, regardless of marital status, is in keeping one's spirit of adventure, love of surprises, and an untiring quest for joy.

> *Empowering Statement:* Romantic experiences are up to me; I am the magician of my own life.

Magic Moment

Anatoly and Tatiana Valushkin have carried their love through continents and years. Their romance survived long distance, financial and other challenges. Yet, in the hardest of times, Tatiana would receive flowers regularly and Anatoly would be welcomed home with hot dinner lovingly made from scratch. Below is one of their many fascinating stories.

"Back then we had a long-distance relationship. We arranged to meet in Chicago and spend a few days together. Late in the afternoon, we arrived at our cozy hotel room, which was perfectly suited for a romantic evening. We were planning to light up candles, fill up a bathtub, intersperse rose petals over it, and take delight in each other. It turned out that we did not have matches, so we went downstairs to get them.

"Many people in the lobby were dressed very formally. Men wore tuxedoes and suits, and women had on evening gowns and heels. In contrast, we looked very casual, as our plan was to return to our room shortly. Some event was clearly happening nearby. Curious, we followed the sound of live music coming out from one of the ballrooms. In a hallway we met a friendly couple who were the attendees of the conference for plastic surgeons. They invited us to attend the reception. We decided to go with the flow and walked into a room filled with dressed-up people, flowers, and a giant, but empty dance floor in the middle.

"Unlike conservative participants of the conference, we were in the mood for dance. We walked into the middle and started spinning in amusement, enjoying the music and each other, as we did not care what was going on around us. Inevitably, we drew attention. The musicians cheered and revived. At first people were watching us, then a few couples joined us on the dance floor, and very soon the entire room was pirouetting, swaying, and boogying.

"When musicians stopped playing, to take a break, people came up to us thanking us for making the evening fun and for inspiring them. Everyone was noticing that we were in love and congratulated us, thinking that we were honeymooners. People were offering us champagne and refreshments. There was a moment when security noticed how different we looked from everyone else and came up to remove us, but the crowd eagerly confirmed that we were guests and asked the guards to leave us alone. We spent a few hours partying and returned to our room well after midnight. We brought in flowers that people gave us. Slightly buzzed and tired, but even happier than before, we lit up our candles, dispersed rose petals over warm foamy water in the bathtub, and finally relaxed into a perfectly romantic Magic Moment."

PART IV

Relationship Vision

Create Your Vision

Everyone who is successful must have dreamed of something.
—Native American Proverb, Maricopa

ow it's time for the fun part! You will be guided through a creative process from which your unique relationship vision will be born and crystallized. This vision will be a continuously evolving goal to guide your course.

Creating a clear picture of what you want, supported by visual representation, is an extremely powerful tool. By focusing on ways to achieve this picture, you will encounter more opportunities than ever before. I invite you to free your mind to dream big and allow your deepest wishes to surface.

Grab a sheet of paper and write down your "why" at the top of the page. Then, with the assumption that anything is possible, take time to answer the questions below. Allow your thoughts to pour as they come, without rationalizing or editing. Use present tense and affirmative statements. Imagine yourself being in the relationship of your dreams with the love of your life. Try to *feel* for responses from your heart and capture them in words the best you can. Most importantly, take pleasure in the process!

Keeping your relationship purpose in mind (your "why") please answer the following questions:

1. What are your mate's values and character traits?
2. What are other characteristics of your partner that are important to you?
3. What are the dynamics of your communication?
4. What is your intimacy like?
5. What kind of experiences are you having together?
6. What is the trust level between the two of you?
7. What do you feel toward your mate?
8. What do you sense your lover is projecting and expressing toward you?
9. Describe your ideal mother in law…just kidding ☺

One of the purposes of this exercise is to provide a "preview" of the feeling of being in an extraordinary relationship, so you know what to look for. Also, you have written down some essential ingredients for your future success. Please note that detailed descriptions of a future mate can be tricky. Our wants are often preconditioned to boost our ego or social status, or to elicit approval from parents and make friends jealous. This can translate into wanting to marry a doctor or date a model, or look for someone with a college degree. It is important to evaluate your vision and separate the wheat from the chaff.

When we become too fixated on certain characteristics, we stop seeing the forest for the trees. We come up with standards and begin measuring people that appear in our lives against these criteria. Often, we get so involved marking things off the checklist that we forget to look into the eyes of the person in front of us and feel his soul.

When I conduct private coaching sessions, I often ask my clients to describe the kind of relationship they would like to be in. Many of them start by automatically giving me the list of desired traits in their future mate instead. By the way, if in your mind you did not catch why this answer is different from what I asked, it means that you fall into the same trap. The kind of relationship means the quality of your experiences within your union—this entails describing "we" or "us." When demand-like requirements for your partner come to the forefront, they obscure your intuitive responses. Therefore, it is much more productive to focus on how you want to feel in a relationship and what you and your lover would be like together.

When acquainting with the mate of your dreams, things like age, nationality, profession, eye color, or place of residence can come as a total surprise and not match the exact portrait you envisioned. It is absolutely necessary to know what you want. At the same time, it is just as vital to be open-minded and flexible, acknowledging the limitations of your current perspective and trusting the Providence to bring what's best for you.

Aleksey is five years younger than I am—something I least expected to happen. Now I am glad this is the case! Joe Dunn always thought that he didn't like redheads; yet, he found Mali, who is a redhead, extremely attractive, and he calls her his soul mate. Dianne and Alan Collins were not each other's "type," which allowed them to be straightforward and honest with each other. Lack of expectations prompted them to develop a profound and sincere connection and behave naturally from the very beginning. Alan said, "The place where we've started is the place where many relationships hope to end up." Life would be too boring if it did not deliver its gifts as a surprise. Be open to receiving and looking inside the package before you make your judgments.

To magnify your relationship vision, to make it more tangible and help you *feel* for it, create a vision board or a journal. Gather pictures from magazines that represent what you wrote, and organize them into an eye-candy collage. Add quotes you resonate with or statements you wrote relating to your vision. Maybe include photos of couples whose relationships inspire you.

Your goal is to enjoy the anticipation and pretend that you already have this amazing romantic union. In your mind, share every beautiful experience with your partner, and imagine stimulating discussions. Kiss her "good-night" before you go to sleep, and wake up smiling, visualizing the love of your life peacefully sleeping next to you. It's as if you booked a vacation to a beautiful place, you've seen the photos and know your itinerary. Yet, there are many unknowns in your journey, and you take pleasure in the thrill of anticipation.

Before I met my husband, I would visualize riding in a car with him, and since I would be driving in the moment, I pictured him on a passenger seat. However, it always raised a question within me as to why would I be driving, if I am with my man. Funny that after I met Aleksey, he would come to visit me in Los Angeles, and naturally I would be driving my car. He was exactly where I envisioned—next to me. My question was answered and my visualization became reality.

Another helpful tool I used was a card I carried in my wallet. To make one, get a rectangular piece of thick paper approximately the size of a business card. On one side write the purpose of your relationship—your "why" statement—and on another, create a bullet list containing the main points from your vision. Laminate it, if you'd like. This helps focus your intent and serves as a reminder of your priorities. When you take a break at work, or while waiting in line, or when you're about to meditate, glance at this card, and feel the warmth in your heart, imagining what it would be like to live your extraordinary romance and passionate love affair of a lifetime.

Magic Moment

It is the day of our arrival in Mexico. We just got settled in a gorgeous condo right on the beach. This will be our home for the next two months. The sun went down, dinner is ready, and we are starting to unwind, sipping crisp and fruity white wine that our hosts kindly left in the fridge. Madeleine Peyroux's velvety voice pleasantly flows from the stereo system and puts the final touch on the perfect evening.

Our romantic solitude is interrupted by the sound of shooting outside. Alarmed, we take a peek through the thick blinds to see what's going on. To our astonishment, spectacular flowers of flame and sparks are bursting against the starry sky—fireworks! We walk out to the balcony. As if just for us, right above our heads, the spectacular display of colored lights continues to unfold. Shiny rain with popping sounds is giving way to single rockets and is then followed by gigantic balls of burning flickers. Fiery glints are taking quaint shapes, which are dissolving in the darkness. It is so close and so beautiful, it took our breath away! What a gift from the benevolent Universe and its Creator!

PART V

The Main
Ingredient – You

Your Key to Happiness

nce upon a time, there lived a prince who inherited the Kingdom of Happiness. However, the keys to its gate were lost. If unlocked, the happiness contained in the kingdom could bring joy and fulfillment to all people, and the prince himself would live an exuberant and blissful life. The prince searched for the keys throughout his empire and asked every person around, to no avail. Finally, he traveled to far-off lands, facing many challenges along the way, but the keys to the Kingdom of Happiness kept eluding him. Lastly, he went to see a woman-sorcerer and asked for advice. Her kind eyes twinkled mischievously, and she inquired, "Have you tried to push the gate open?" The prince was flustered with surprise: "No...I mean, I thought it was locked." The old woman laughed and sighed. "You went too far to look for your answers; they are always within. Your *intention* is your key. Claim your Kingdom, as you alone decide how wide the gate will open and how much happiness will flow out into the world."

This section is dedicated to the main component of your relationship—*you*. Your beliefs, your attitudes, your fears, your desires, and your perception of yourself and of the world around you shape your experience. Full control of your relationship success is in your hands. And it is not fifty-fifty, where you are accountable for half and your partner is in charge of the other half. The entire one hundred percent is up to you. This may seem outrageous, but think about it. Who invites a romantic partner into your life? You make a choice whom to be with. Who evokes certain qualities and behaviors in your mate? You do.

Have you noticed how various aspects of your own personality surface depending on whom you are interacting with? For example, are there people in your life who think you are terrific and have plenty of nice things to say about you? At the same time, is there somebody who is critical of you and can easily list your shortcomings and poor choices? Do you conduct yourself differently with these people?

Each one of us has a wide palette of responses to people and situations, ranging from love to violence. Which one of them we choose to express in the moment depends on two factors: our overall state—physical, mental and emotional—and the stimuli we receive from other people. We can be very sensitive to the influences of others, which usually triggers knee-jerk reactions. However, when we are centered and confident, we become an influencer, which prompts us to offer conscious and deliberate responses. This means that you are the creative genius behind your love story. And your life experiences are merely a reflection of your inner world.

If you are a woman[3], in essence you are a beautiful princess yearning to open her heart and completely surrender to true love. If you are a man[4], at your core you are a courageous warrior who is ready to face death and defeat the enemy for the sake of love. Unfortunately, life experiences often turn heroes into wimps, and princesses into ball-busters. Hostage to our own fears and insecurities, we put on masks and adopt behaviors that lead us apart from our true nature.

---

3   A person with a predominant feminine essence, regardless of actual gender
4   A person with a predominant masculine essence

In the following chapters, I invite you to connect with your real essence and defuse the illusions that have kept you guarding your soul. If you are a woman, I want your radiant beauty and femininity to come to the forefront. If you are a man, let's awaken your powerful spirit and discover your purpose and drive.

First, let me share another episode from my experience, which led me to a remarkable discovery.

Navigating Out
of the Turmoil

y three-year-long relationship fell apart. Even though I was the one who walked away, it still felt like a failure. I was deeply disappointed in myself, in my ex, and in the whole idea of "happily ever after." Breakups are exhausting. A history of arguments, attempts to start over, and the process of final separation were an immense drain of emotional energy. We were living together, so I was moving out and starting from scratch. A shadow of myself, I couldn't even remember the last time I'd laughed out loud. I wanted to feel lighthearted and joyful, but instead it felt like I was dragging a heavy burden. I longed to return to my normal self, to have my own personality back, to joke, to be playful, and to be happy. I had fallen into a common trap thinking that I should adjust who I am in order to suit the needs of our relationship, that I should sacrifice and modify my habits and preferences to be "easier to live with." What a huge mistake. It was a guarantee for disaster.

Yet I knew that I had to find peace and courage within myself in order to expect a brighter future. I thought of doing something that I love. Dancing had been one of my favorite forms of self-expression since childhood, so I decided to take lessons.

The board on the wall of the 3rd Street Dance Studio listed upcoming classes in salsa, ballroom, ballet, and Argentine tango. *Argentine tango*! That sounded passionate and fun. Who could have imagined that it would turn into an amazingly powerful and transformational journey?

Tango Therapy

*While I dance I cannot judge, I cannot hate, I
cannot separate myself from life. I can only be
joyful and whole. This is why I dance.*
—Hans Bos

Argentine tango is a language, and it bears a peculiar resemblance to relationship dynamics in real life. Music inspires communication. The partners become a single entity uniquely expressing passion, drama, and bliss for the duration of a song. A tango couple is usually perceived as a man leading a woman, but it is also common to see two men or two women dancing. Sometimes pairs switch roles, and the woman takes the lead… just like in life. Always, however, someone has to lead, and another has to follow.

A strong leader is creative, confident, and has a good sense of rhythm. He anticipates the upcoming notes in the music and directs his partner into movement perfectly on the beat. The leader is responsible for the couple's safety on the dance floor and for being considerate of other dancers. Being a great leader requires focus, presence, skill, sensitivity, and perfect timing. Sounds easy, right? It takes guts, accountability, and passion…just what it takes to be a real man.

My breakup had shaken my confidence in men. It was challenging for me to relax on the dance floor and let someone else be in charge. I was stiff and tried to control the motion. However, as I practiced to become a better dancer, my psychological blocks dissolved. The more I could relax and become "light," the more I was able to see men outside of the dance floor as trustworthy. Or maybe it worked the other way around; who knows? But what became certain was that my body acted out my emotional state.

Following the lead requires trusting yourself to pick the right partner and, after the choice is made, relaxing completely and feeling for direction. It also leaves room to improvise. Sometimes you can intentionally refuse to go with the lead, offering your own movement instead. It makes the dance more interesting and the dynamic less predictable, making it an adventure for both.

Good dancers are picky in choosing a partner. One of my tango teachers once told me, "You have to think of yourself as a Stradivarius violin—you cannot let just anyone play you; only skillful masters should place such a fine instrument into their hands. Bad partners will put you out of tune and rip your stings."

However, before you learn how to pick the right partner, you have to become finely tuned yourself. The steps below will serve as a tuning fork and align you with your relationship vision. They will lay a solid foundation for a lasting relationship success.

10 Steps to Becoming a Great Partner

So what does it take to be a great partner on and off the dance floor? First, you have to be available to dance. It seems obvious, but it's easier said than done. Most people carry a heavy burden of their past relationships, along with the resulting emotional distress. Often, it goes far back into childhood, starting with their parents. In order to flow freely on the dance floor of life, we have to strip down the fictitious layers, shake off fears and heavy burdens, open our hearts, and courageously take the lead or trustingly follow.

Shall we dance?

Step 1

Accept Yourself

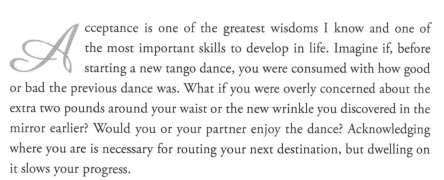

cceptance is one of the greatest wisdoms I know and one of the most important skills to develop in life. Imagine if, before starting a new tango dance, you were consumed with how good or bad the previous dance was. What if you were overly concerned about the extra two pounds around your waist or the new wrinkle you discovered in the mirror earlier? Would you or your partner enjoy the dance? Acknowledging where you are is necessary for routing your next destination, but dwelling on it slows your progress.

Acceptance sets you free by putting you in a state of harmony with yourself and the world, and by removing the blocks that obscure the radiance of love from your heart. We resist the flow of life by resenting things in ourselves, in our physical bodies, in others, in external situations, and in the world at large.

On the dance floor this translates into stiffness, lack of confidence, and lack of creativity. In your body, it shows up as muscle tensions, chronic conditions, and an array of other stress-related symptoms. In your life situation, it manifests as misfortunes, problems, and even accidents.

We simply have no choice but to accept our physical condition, current state of affairs, and past experiences as a fact. A brighter and better future can be created from this point forward. Judging, criticizing, blaming, or labeling the existing circumstances as "wrong" is simply a waste of resources.

Accustomed to categorizing things as "good" or "bad," we develop a sense of separation between ourselves and others, between our current situation and the ideal to which we aspire, between spirituality and the physical world, and between God and people. This symptom is understandable, because we can clearly distinguish a ripe juicy apple from a rotten one, and since the immediate benefits of the former are obvious to us, we call it "good." Yet, we fail to recognize that decomposition is a necessary part of the cycle of life. It feeds microorganisms, supplies nutrients for the soil, and provides favorable conditions for seed germination, which, in turn, promotes new life and assures future harvests. Take this process away, and soon there will be no apples. Shouldn't we stop calling a rotten apple "bad?" In nature all processes are interdependent, and in your life, all events are interrelated, too.

Every solution is born of a problem, every advancement springs from discontent, and every achievement is a result of a challenge. Praising one and condemning another is equal to denying a part of existence. If back in the day our ancestors weren't limited by darkness at night, they wouldn't be stimulated to invent candles and, later, electricity. If life didn't present its challenges to you, you wouldn't be as strong as you are today. Your triumph is always as sweet as the bitterness of the battle you are fighting. Neutralize the antagonistic forces within by making peace with all aspects of your own life. Bless your mistakes as much as you bless your successes. Appreciate your difficulties like you appreciate your luck. Embrace your weaknesses similarly as you would your talents. Accept challenges as stimuli for growth, and look for the next opportunity. Celebrate your next victory, and then plan and execute the next step. To experience wholeness, you have to accept and embrace the whole of you and the whole of life.

Unfortunately, labeling is a cornerstone of our society, which makes it difficult to see past the initial judgments and to grasp the bigger picture. It is helpful to acknowledge that every opinion reflects only one point of view, while there are myriad perspectives. What seems to be "bad" today can turn out to be a "blessing" tomorrow, and "good luck" can reverse into a "curse."

Would you consider a car breaking down to be unfortunate? Well, if in July 1926 Napoleon Hill's car had not broken down, he would've been murdered for trying to bring Prohibition gangsters to justice. The world would've never seen the greatest self-improvement book of all time, *Think and Grow Rich*, and millions of people would not have been touched by it.

We believe it is horrible when a nine-year-old child dies in a car accident. But doesn't it bring another perspective when you learn that this incident inspired a movement, warmed thousands of hearts, and made a major difference in the lives of over sixty thousand people? Rachel Beckwith's dream to help children of Africa took on a life of its own after the girl departed our physical dimension. Her charity raised over $1.26 million and funded 149 wells supplying clean water to the communities of Ethiopia. The purity of Rachel's intent and the generosity of her spirit continue to live, encouraging others and making a difference.

Things are rarely the way they appear. Not every glittery thing is gold, and not every disaster is a misfortune. In reality, our ups and downs are symbiotic and should be embraced equally. Life is whole, and the processes of the Universe are inseparable. Acceptance does not mean approving things you disagree with or liking something unpleasant. It does not entail giving up or ceasing to seek improvement either. It means finding an inner peace despite any undesirable circumstances. Once you look for things to appreciate in the midst of adversity, you will be able to see tranquility in the eye of a tornado and allow *Infinite Intelligence* to guide your way.

No matter where you find yourself today, life can turn around in a blink of an eye. There is always more fun, more love, and new experiences around the corner. The next song will bring new inspiration and unforeseen unfolding. Even the most hostile and hopeless situations carry a seed of new opportunity.

Years ago, a relative of mine returned home to discover her husband in bed with another woman. Crushed and devastated, she stormed out of the

The widespread tendency to point fingers and blame everyone and their mother, but to never look in the mirror, can be easily explained. For most of us, the feeling of self-worth is linked to our accomplishments and the opinions of others about us. Since we were kids, we sought out the attention and love of our parents, which was vital to our well-being. Whether we were praised and rewarded, or reprimanded and punished depended on our behavior. So we learned early on that we can be "good" or "bad." We also concluded that good things in life, including love, have to be deserved, just like our favorite ice cream or cookie.

Consequently, any perceived shortcoming or fault presents a potential threat to our sense of dignity. We fear that our flaws or inadequacies will lead to being disliked, rejected, and forsaken. Because we are social creatures and being part of a group assured our survival for millennia, we seek approval of others at all costs.

Love is the fuel of our soul. The fear of not being good enough to deserve love drives our attempts to find excuses, or accuse or denounce others. We instinctively redirect the dangerous force of criticism, trying to preserve our own good face even at the price of devaluing others. Whenever possible, we eagerly blame situations, events, and conditions, gladly diminishing our own role in the final outcome.

However, any advancement or achievement we highly regard springs from daring to be different and trying new things. This inevitably involves failed attempts and objections. Any jump in evolution at first appears as a freak of nature, before it proves to be stronger, more adept, and enduring.

According to the prominent cellular biologist Bruce H. Lipton, PhD, survival of life organisms is assured by two fundamental behaviors: protection and growth. However, these functions cannot be performed simultaneously. In his book *Biology of Belief* Dr. Lipton writes: "It turns out that the mechanisms that support growth and protection cannot operate optimally at the same time. In other words, cells cannot simultaneously move forward and backward. The human blood vessel cells I studied at Stanford exhibited one microscopic anatomy for providing nutrition and a completely different microscopic anatomy for providing a protection response.

In a response similar to that displayed by cells, humans unavoidably restrict their growth behaviors when they shift into a protective mode. If you're running from a mountain lion, it's not a good idea to expend energy on growth. In order to survive—that is, escape the lion—you summon all your energy for your fight-or-flight response. Redistributing energy reserves to fuel the protection response inevitably results in a curtailment of growth." Hollywood movies that portray superheroes making love in the midst of running for their life are inaccurate, to say the least. That is because escaping requires activation of the protection mechanisms; lovemaking, on the other hand, is geared toward procreation and pleasure and, therefore, calls for growth mode.

Meeting the *one* and creating a wonderful life together requires you to be in the growth mode. Blames and excuses are protective forces, which will close you off and stand in the way of sincere communication. Therefore, your willingness to recognize the direct correlation between your choices and your outcomes is crucial.

When you acknowledge that your disappointments are products of your decisions, you can learn from them and make better choices in the future. When you are constantly complaining and offsetting your responsibility onto someone or something else, you turn into your own enemy by relinquishing your own command and wasting the opportunity to grow.

> *Never think there is anything impossible for the soul. It is the*
> *greatest heresy to think so. If there is sin, this is the only sin—to say*
> *that you are weak, or others are weak.*
> —Swami Vivekananda

Owning your results requires audacity and honesty. Yet, it helps you claim the immense power, which is your birthright. It elevates you from a pitiful victim into a genius creator who is in charge of her own life. True love requires taking accountability. A great relationship calls for courage, sincerity, and vulnerability.

Step 3

Clean Out the Closet

*You cannot protect yourself from sadness
without protecting yourself from happiness.*
—Jonathan Safran Foer, *Extremely Loud and Incredibly Close*[5]

Every new dance has to have a fresh start so that you can relax, become one with your new partner, and allow the music to captivate you. Focusing on how your former partner stepped on your toe and how it still hurts will ruin the enchantment of the experience. It's your job to heal your pains of the past prior to embracing a new person. Your complete presence in full capacity and devotion are essential for an utterly satisfying and memorable dance.

A magical relationship requires you to be completely open with your partner. Past traumas or unresolved issues will support your fears and keep you in the protection mode. Any time your current interaction with your

---

5   First published by Houghton Mifflin Harcourt, 2005

lover remotely resembles the preceding painful events, your mind will raise the warning signs and trigger your defensive responses. This can prompt you to act wary and get in the way of true intimacy. It is vital to let go of this baggage and start with a clean slate. This prerequisite is rooted in your very biology. The results of an extensive research at Stanford conducted by Dr. Lipton confirmed that "Growth processes require an open exchange between an organism and its environment. For example, food is taken in and waste products are excreted. However, protection requires a closing down of the system to wall the organism off from the perceived threat." (*Biology of Belief,* Hay House 2008)

Your body is supported by the constant stream of life energy flowing through you. Suppressed negative emotions, stressful experiences, or unexpressed thoughts get trapped in your body's tissues, creating "obstacles" to the free flow of energy. Scientists and doctors have come up with different terms to describe this phenomenon: "energy cysts"[6] or "trapped energy,"[7] and developed various techniques to discharge them.

While many of these energy-release approaches require a licensed practitioner, there are also powerful and easy-to-learn self-help methods. I will share with you several practical tools that I've successfully applied for years.

Shrink in a Faucet
Shrink in a Faucet is a highly effective and very simple process that I have developed. It can be equally helpful in resolving long-standing inner conflicts and small in-the-moment irritations. You can do it almost anywhere any time. It will help you reduce your stress level dramatically. Also, it will benefit every relationship you have—in your home, at your work place, with friends, and even with perfect strangers.

---

6   Dr. Elmer Green observed the work of Dr. Upledger and Dr. Zvarni and suggested the term 'energy cyst' "SomatoEmotional Release: Deciphering the Language of Life" John E. Upledger, Richard Grossinger
7   Emotion Code: How to Release Your Trapped Emotions for Abundant Health, Love and Happiness Bradley B. Nelson

When stressful situations occur, we often try to remain decent through restricting our knee-jerk reactions and suppressing negative emotions. This way people around us do not have to be subjected to our moods. However, this very tactic is largely responsible for accumulating tensions in the body's tissues. Over time it may lead to stress-related illnesses, anxiety, or depression. It is important to provide an outlet for negative impulses and discharge them as soon as they appear. This is where Shrink in a Faucet comes handy. Use it whenever you are faced with undesirable circumstances that cause you distress: disappointment, annoyance, frustration, resentment, blame, etc.

When your mind is racing, and expressing your feelings is not an option, go to the bathroom or any other place with running water (kitchen, fountain, garden irrigation, brook, ocean, and so on). Make sure you are alone, so you are not written off as a nutcase, because things you are about to voice are not for anyone else's ears. With the open water running, and with the intent to release your inner resistance and all accompanied emotions, ramble out everything you have to say. Speak out your concerns, anger, or rage. Water will play the role of your offender or a psychoanalyst, whichever you prefer. It is a good time for name calling and cursing, if that is how you feel. Water can take it all and carry it away, so be generous and hold nothing back. Even if you are in a public place and raising your voice is not possible, still mumble everything under your breath and let it out. You can even do it in a stall and flush afterwards. However, it is important to use water, because it stores and carries information. That said, I do not recommend using the shower when you are in it.

Doing something like this sounds silly, I know. Would you rather look silly and be happy, or appear smart and be stressed? This simple tool works, because it not only helps you remain sane and balanced; it also protects the people around you. You might refrain from voicing your unflattering opinion to your boss, but the people close to you will have to hear it instead. How often do we abuse others with useless and unpleasant mind vomits? We tell our family members or coworkers how bad the traffic was or how long we had to wait in line, how difficult it was to find parking, or how we were mistreated. By sharing these things we simply pass our stresses onto others.

Instead of burdening your loved ones at the expense of their health, or your shrink at the rate of three hundred dollars per hour, release your baggage for free. Water is a fabulous friend, who can take it all, including things you have never told anyone and been carrying around for years. Let them out of your body and out of your life experience for good.

In personal relationships this simple practice is invaluable. It helps me regularly. If I get upset, before I talk to my husband, I release the emotional charge around the subject. This helps our conversation to be constructive and solution-oriented, as opposed to an argumentative or heated discussion.

Emotional Freedom Technique (EFT)

Emotional Freedom Technique is an energy balancing method developed by Gary Craig. It addresses a variety of issues rooted in emotional causes: phobias, traumas, anger, guilt, grief, performance challenges, and a number of physical symptoms, including pains. The method incorporates the body's energy meridians, which are the focus of Eastern healing practices and traditionally used in acupuncture and acupressure. First, EFT prompts you to focus on the issue you would like to resolve. Then you tap with your fingertips on the meridian points in your body. According to Gary Craig, this helps to remove energy disruptions and restores the normal flow of energy, which, in turn, eliminates the problem. I think it's best that you learn this technique from the source; therefore, I am not including the manual. You can find the detailed guide on how to perform EFT and related information at www.emofree.com. It is free, very easy to grasp, and a very helpful tool to have in your arsenal. As far as I know, there are no side effects.

I learned EFT many years ago and it has proved to be effective time and again. I was able to help my husband, myself, and those around me, to relieve headaches, minor pains, hiccups, and to ease emotional burdens of the past. I helped my father cure his extreme fear of heights, which he had had for over fifty years. It went away after only one session! A few weeks later, we had a chance to test the results. My dad went zip lining from the highest mountains in Costa Rica…and loved it!

EFT is not a panacea and does not work in every case. However, I have had enough successes using it to confidently recommend it. Explore it for yourself, and draw your own conclusions on its effectiveness.

Breaking the Ties to Your Exes

The images of your previous lovers or unfulfilled dreams, and the emotional sorrows linked to them can also cloud the purity of your love with your current or future partner. It is essential to let go of all links to your exes. This means a firm decision in your heart to move on—passing the point of no return.

When we get into a relationship with another person, connecting intimately, we literally form a third entity, which is neither you nor your partner, but a couple—"we" and "us." Sometimes a relationship falls apart, but the bond to this third entity remains intact; and in our thoughts, fantasies, and memories, we trace it back. It continues to hold us, not allowing a clear connection to the new mate. Often, one partner is completely detached, but another stays emotionally involved. However, this causes sorrows for both. The partner who remains linked starts acting

IT'S NOT THAT I DON'T LOVE YOU, I DO. MY EX WAS JUST MORE PHOTOGENIC.

weird, obsessive, and sometimes even violent. And the partner who moved on feels laden and irritated by the attempts of the former to restore the relationship. Pretty much everyone has been on one or another side of this lopsided equation.

In other cases, both partners cannot let go of these ties, even if a relationship is clearly not working. As a result, they go through continuous episodes of splitting up and getting back together. Some even divorce and later marry the same person. It's like being stuck on a roller coaster ride… exciting at first, but sickening in the long run.

One of my acquaintances had this type of attachment to her on-and-off boyfriend. They dragged out the ongoing drama for over ten years, constantly breaking up and making up. She would complain about him discouraging her, putting her down, and verbally abusing her. She would swear to put an end to it, but would always find a legitimate reason to give their relationship another try. She would flirt with other men and go out on dates, and would even have passionate romances followed by heartbreaks. Then, she would always return to the painful, but familiar "home base."

People take strange enjoyment in melodramatic situations like this. They hide from loneliness behind the twisted romance. It affords them attention and compassion of others, which makes them feel valued and significant.

Achieving full closure requires only your intention. There is no need to communicate with your exes. You can free yourself in three easy steps:

1. Firmly decide to let go of all ties to your previous romantic partners.
2. Appreciate former mates and relationships as learning experiences and stepping-stones on your way to the love of your life. Every ex has contributed to who you have become, and to your current aims. You have faced challenges together, shared good times, made mistakes, and learned vital lessons. They have inspired clarity and new desires in you. If they gave you children, that is a divine gift to appreciate.
3. Release all ties, using the meditative technique below.

I created this meditation for myself not long before I met my husband. I knew the importance of removing all attachments that were no longer serving me. It was a necessary step in making me emotionally available.

If you don't know how to meditate, the detailed information and the introduction to meditation are available for free at www.BestThingEver.com.

There is also a complimentary recording of a guided meditation designed for relaxation, stress relief, and for honing your meditation skills.

Breaking the Ties to Ex-lovers Meditation

Sit comfortably in a quiet place; turn on relaxing music, if you like. Take a few deep breaths while relaxing your muscles. Imagine being in a soothing and enjoyable place: on a beach, in a forest meadow, or in a tree house. Remember the very first attraction in your life. Was it your neighbor, a kindergarten mate, or a special someone from school? Invite him or her to join you in your ideal place of relaxation. Visualizing this person in front of you, notice your feelings toward him. If it evokes a positive response in you, like amusement, thank him mentally for fulfilling his purpose in your life, and then say goodbye forever. Repeat the process, inviting your romantic interests one after another in chronological order, moving from the past to the present day. If anyone conjures tension or resentment in you, focus on the benefits this relationship has had in your life. Recall the good experiences you had together, and be thankful for new understandings this person has inspired in you. Did you start making better decisions because of the lessons you learned through your interactions? Look for things to appreciate in your journey with this ex until your inner resistance subsides. Let your intuition guide this process. If you have trouble forgiving or letting go of resentment, ask your spiritual guides[8] for help. Then relax and listen; the right idea will come. When you manage to discharge your negative emotions and start feeling neutral toward this person, tell him or her: "You were a perfect match for me then, and I appreciate that you played your role so well. I am in a different place now, and you are no longer necessary. I release you permanently, with blessings." The feeling of relief is your indicator of a successful release. To get out of the meditative state, count from one to five, and slowly open your eyes.

---

8   Non-physical entity of higher consciousness

Releasing the ties and forgiving may be more difficult in some cases than others. I felt so much disgust toward one of my ex-boyfriends that visualizing him triggered a strong negative response in me. After a few attempts, I decided to imagine his *divine* essence instead of focusing on the image of his physical appearance. It worked amazingly well! I almost felt him being my spiritual brother, and then I was able to feel appreciation for his contributions into my personal evolution. After all, I chose to be with him at the time; he never promised to fulfill my every expectation.

Assume control of your past relationships. You were always in charge of your choices, and you were calling the shots. Even if the results of the past did not please you, the freedom to make wiser decisions going forward is yours irrevocably. You may require a few of these sessions to let go of all emotional attachments. But I promise you it will be an incredibly liberating and elating experience.

A different approach is required if you feel yearning for one of your former mates, but this desire is not mutual or you cannot be together for whatever reason. In this case your longing is the result of your idealizing this person and/or limiting thoughts that no one better can come along. Very often, it is your own hidden fear of being not good enough playing out in the world. To compensate for this insecurity, your ego demands evidence that you are worthy of being loved, and the proof must come from the person who is less likely to give you affection or commitment. It is a subconscious game of your own mind masterfully concealed with an ostensibly valid rationale. In your head, you merge the image of this person with the ideal mate you dreamed of, completely disregarding obvious incompatibilities, even the fact that your desired partner should cherish you and love you wholeheartedly. However, because you have trouble loving yourself unconditionally and constantly put harsh demands upon yourself, and eat yourself alive with self-criticism every time your own standards are not met, you conclude that it's normal for another person not to accept you for simply who you are.

Typically this starts in childhood when one of our parents pays less attention to us or gives us less warmth or praise than the other parent. We try especially hard to get approval and love from that parent. Some people dedicate their entire life to gaining the respect of their mother or father. Ironically, they never get what they are hoping for, because the bar gets raised higher and higher and they always fall short of reaching it. In truth, it is not the approval of others—be it parents or lovers—that you are seeking, but the feeling of wholeness, where your ego cannot discount any part of you and hinder the flow of love through your being. As soon as you stop placing limitations on loving yourself and embrace and value yourself fully, you will become whole and free of draining connections. It is crucial to understand that any unrequited love, whichever form it takes, is simply your ego's attempt to boost its self-worth. This is why playing "hard to get" can be effective for getting temporary attention, because the ego of the pursuer automatically starts chasing its tail.

In order to free yourself from clinging to ghosts, first you have to look soberly at this partner and your experience with her and weigh it against your relationship purpose and vision. Second, you need to acknowledge that there are infinite opportunities and open up to them. The meditation below is designed specifically for disengaging from ill-natured longings.

Releasing Lopsided Connections Meditation

Sit comfortably or lie down and get into a meditative state. In your mind's eye go to a pleasant place to relax, be it a forest meadow, beach, or riverbank, etc. Stay there for a while soaking up the colors, fragrances, and textures of the surroundings. Before you invite the person you want to disconnect from to join you, know that his life took a vastly different course since the last time you saw him, and be ready for a surprise. Imagine in front of you a folding screen. The subject of your yearning will appear behind it. Call this person forth. Now the invisible force will slowly lift the screen revealing this obsession of yours gradually. The screen starts moving upward and first you see feet wearing flip-flops with ridiculously long toenails that haven't been clipped for months. Then purple with horizontal yellow striped trousers appear. Then, a green shirt with red polka dots is revealed. As the screen is completely lifted, you notice that this person's hair is died bright pink, and he is picking his nose. Address him by name and very congenially thank him for his contribution into your life. Tell him that you wish him well, but your paths are too different now and you no longer wish to be with him. When you are ready, ask him to leave your mind, your heart, and your life forever. Feel relief and freedom.

When you are alone again, feel warmth toward the lover who is waiting to become your devoted life partner. Connect to this person through your heart. Feel the response and affection coming toward you. Let the *one* know that your heart is now available and open to welcome him. Tell him that you are now ready to receive and embrace him completely and you look forward to gazing into his beautiful eyes for the first time. Promise that you will keep your heart and your soul pure and will prepare for the meeting in the meantime. Send a kiss to your future mate. Trust that he is dreaming of you just the same. From now on, any time you feel an aching yearning for connection, allow your heart to reach for his and know that you will always feel loved in return. Slowly come out of the meditative state.

It is much easier to practice these processes when they are guided. For your convenience, I have produced audio recordings with all the meditations narrated and explained. To get your copy or to obtain more information, go to www.BestThingEver.com.

Step 4

Weed Out
Limiting Beliefs

y husband loves taking pictures, and he has a very good Nikon camera. As we traveled to exotic destinations, he captured the astonishing beauty we witnessed. Unfortunately, the majority of the photographs looked quite dull compared to what our eyes perceived. He tried to adjust the settings, find better angles, and every other trick that came to mind. The pictures remained rather bleak still. Finally, he asked a friend—a professional photographer—for advice. It turned out that the camera needed a different filter. The difference in quality of the shots with the new filter was amazing. The images finally reflected the true vibrancy of the colors.

You experience the world through the filters of your beliefs. Your outlook in life is screened through your perceptions and determined by what you choose to focus on. The world around you can be gorgeous, but if your views are limiting, you will see a gloomy picture.

Your beliefs are the blueprint for your life. "As within, so without," says Hermetic philosophy. This passage suggests that your inner world is recreated in your experiences. I am sure you have heard of *The Law of Attraction*: "Like attracts like." This means that *The Law of Attraction* will match you up with your own truth, and every belief you hold will be supported by plenty of evidence. However, if your convictions are not conducive to your happiness, you may not like this evidence.

For instance, if you think that all men sooner or later cheat, you will receive plenty of confirmation for your belief. It will be painful and disappointing every time. Interestingly, this has nothing to do with the validity of your conviction. If you thought that men were loyal and capable of commitment, you would receive confirmation of that.

Your beliefs are also reflected in the quality of your relationship. Therefore, you have to identify which perceptions about yourself, about your potential partner and intimacy contradict your relationship vision. Then, replace them with more empowering perspectives that are beneficial for long-term success.

A belief is an assertion that you consider to be true. Beliefs stem from the meanings we assign to our life experiences. Events and circumstances are neutral until our mind makes sense out of them. "Snow," for example, is a natural phenomenon, but for everyone it means something unique. For a person who lives in a Northern country and has to shovel it every day during winter, snow can mean "work." For an avid skier who travels to get fresh powder and explore new slopes, snow means "adventure." For someone who lives in a tropical climate and has never seen or touched snow, it means "miracle." For someone else this word can bring up a warm memory of playing with a parent and mean "love." A belief is formed when we assign the same meaning to a similar circumstance over and over again. For example, some people believe that a certain shirt or a pair of jeans is lucky. This may come as a result of favorable events lining up on several occasions when a person wore this particular garment. For that person this conviction is valid, and for someone else it may seem silly. Therefore, we each hold our own truth. As a society, we arrive to some similar conclusions and agree on common meanings. Different cultures, however, can make opposite assumptions and, consequently, adopt completely different belief systems. In reality, *beliefs are neither true nor false; instead, they are conducive to, or hindering the outcomes you desire.* They are like seeds: whatever you plant will grow and produce corresponding fruits—your results. The opinions we form, the conclusions we draw, and consequent decisions we make are the colors in which we paint our lives. Whatever you choose to believe will compile into your personal truth and govern your reality.

To better illustrate this, let me share with you a true story from my practice.

A client of mine struggled with jealousy. When his girlfriend was communicating with other men, he felt like he "did not exist." I asked him to recall the first time in his life he felt this way. He remembered an episode from his childhood when he was friends with a girl next door, and they were inseparable. One day he introduced his older brother to this girl. Soon after, she became friends with the older brother and abandoned my client. It crushed and devastated him. As a child with a broken heart, he drew many disserving conclusions from this situation. If put into words, they might sound something like this:

- I am not good enough. Just being myself is not enough for girls.
- Girls (women) cannot be trusted.
- Girls prefer my brother; he is better than I am.
- My brother can take away from me what's dear to my heart.
- I can interest a pretty girl, but as soon as she is presented with a better opportunity, she will leave me.

This incident caused a strong emotional experience—the very first step to creating a powerful conviction. These assumptions produced the feelings of powerlessness, inferiority, insecurity, distrust, disappointment, and frustration—all linked to relationships. It is obvious how something like this could affect his confidence and produce many fears. Always precise, *The Law of Attraction* matched up these feelings with more evidence. Later in life this man experienced infidelity, and several other women left him for his older brother. His beliefs grew stronger every time.

Being a very bright man, he could acknowledge that his present-day concerns about his girlfriend were hardly valid. Yet, unresolved sorrows of the past were triggering the protection mode and provoking him to respond adversely. The meanings he assigned to the first incident were painful, and the issue remained unresolved. If my client had arrived at different conclusions, his life events would have unfolded in a completely different way.

Perhaps, instead, he could decide that:

- The girl who deserves my heart is loyal. *This one was not good enough for me.*
- I am sorry for my brother that he got "leftovers."
- If she did not appreciate my caring for her, she sure does not deserve my tears. I will do better next time, and she will be sorry she left me.
- I want a girl who loves and values me for who I am. It will be so much fun when I meet her.
- She is free to make her own decisions. My happiness depends on *my decisions.*
- If it did not work out between us, it means there is someone better for me out there.

Some of these statements are not necessarily kind, but they are more empowering and would get the job done and produce confidence and optimism about the future. They would support greater feelings of self-worth and generate more pleasant life experiences.

Each one of us has experienced situations that have produced a tangled mess of detrimental beliefs. In order to sort them out, we have to get out of our own head and rise above the circumstances to gain access to more perspectives and derive more productive meanings. Life persistently presents its lessons until they are learned, the empowering conclusions are drawn, and the emotional charges are released. The good news is that it is never too late to go back and weed out unfavorable beliefs and plant more beneficial ideas.

To heal similar cases, I recommend the following process:

- Write down the original conclusions you drew from a traumatic episode. In order to formulate them, ask yourself what it meant. Repeat the same question a few times asking, "Besides that, what did it imply?" and record all the different answers that come.
- Come up with a list of alternative meanings. If you struggle with this step, tell your story—you don't have to say it is yours—to other people, and ask what they think this episode means. What kind of conclusions would they arrive at, if they were in your place? The variety of responses will astonish you.
- Pick a few new perspectives that make you feel relieved and confident.
- Do the following meditative exercise.

Releasing Limiting Beliefs Meditation

Get into a meditative state, and play the situation on the imaginary movie screen. See yourself going through emotional turmoil. As "present-day you," step into the picture and approach your former self. Give yourself a hug and lovingly offer a fresh perspective on this incident. Provide support and counsel until you know that your former self is comforted. Connect heart to heart with yourself from the past, feel appreciation for the valuable lesson this occurrence has taught you, and express gratitude to yourself for learning it and using it to become stronger and wiser.

Often, however, we are unaware of our limiting beliefs. They rule our life like an invisible puppeteer. How can you identify them? I'd like to share a simple process with you, which is helpful in uncovering hidden convictions and is designed specifically for interpersonal relationships.

Below is a list of statements. When you read each one of them, observe your reaction closely. You can agree with the statement, disagree, or be unsure. Read the statement, mark your response on a sheet of paper ("yes," "no," or "not sure"), and write a few sentences in support of your point of view starting with the word "because."

- I am creating an amazing, lasting, intimate relationship in my life
- My age is perfect for meeting the right partner
- I deserve to be loved and adored
- Now is the perfect time to get romantically involved
- I can trust my intimate partner and rely on his/her support
- A great personal relationship is beneficial to my career success
- A lasting relationship offers depth and happiness, which can never be found in a short-lived affair
- By creating a blissful relationship, I have nothing to lose, but so much to gain
- A committed relationship is fun and gets better over time
- I can have a life partner and maintain my own independence

Any statement that evoked a response other than "yes" indicates a potential constraint you have set for yourself. Examine your results and create a list of beliefs that hinder your ability to achieve the desired outcome. Usually, each limiting belief is the complete opposite of the statement with which you disagreed. For instance, if you resisted the idea of having a romantic partner while maintaining your own independence, this means you are afraid that you will lose your personal freedom in a devoted partnership. Your limiting thought would be something like: "I might lose my independence if I commit."

Replacing all unfavorable convictions with empowering ones can require some time and discipline. For starters, commit to changing just one. Choose the statement that evoked the least resentment in you. Starting with something easy will help you grasp the technique and give you encouraging results. Recall the experiences that led you to this conclusion. Your answer in the "because" column most likely contains a few hints.

Ask yourself, "What else could this incident mean?" Come up with a list of different views on the same situation, and assign alternative meanings to the event. If an incident involved an offender, try to see this scenario from her perspective. Evaluate every new meaning with your gut, until you find the one that gives you a feeling of relief. Embrace it!

Write down a concise statement—a new belief that you are adopting. It has to ring true at some level. Support it with a few sentences on why this new belief makes sense; add facts and observations, if you can. Commit one minute a day to practice and acquire this new conviction for thirty days. Every morning and every evening, when you are in the bathroom, stand straight in front of a mirror and repeat your new belief, with confidence, three times out loud. This should take only twenty seconds—a very modest price to pay for a life-changing result. Also, stay tuned to the subject, and every time life presents you with a confirmation of your new conviction, acknowledge it and say, "It's true!" and state your new belief. The Law of Attraction will provide plenty of evidence. Before the thirty days are over, you will be inseparable from your empowering perspective and will have trouble remembering what the old one was.

You can repeat the process with other limiting thoughts that occupy your mind. It is a very simple yet effective exercise. It requires your focus and powerful intent. Since our lives are filled with distractions and a continuous stream of information, the best results are achieved when working on *one belief at a time.*

Step 5

Find Your Balance

One of the most crucial skills in Argentine tango is the ability to maintain balance. Each partner has to keep his own balance while paying keen attention to another. This means that if one of the dancers is removed, the other can remain stable on the dance floor. Of course, a stronger man can support a woman who leans on him too much. However, he will have to carry part of her weight, and she will be "heavy to dance with." A man who is out of balance will be constantly throwing the woman off balance as well, regardless of her ability to hold steady. For the longevity and sustainability of a couple, both partners must confidently hold their own ground.

If you look for someone to support you or for someone who can heal your emotional wounds, that means you are limping and are hoping to find a partner who will make you look graceful on the dance floor. Such a union will inevitably be lopsided, and your dance will be an ugly dragging into eventual exhaustion and separation. It will be painful to watch and certainly won't inspire anyone.

Strong couples are formed by strong partners. One of the tango masters shared with me a very symbolic detail about the tango embrace. Great dancers slightly uplift each other by pressing up with the hand on the partner's back. This support is very subtle and offered equally by both dancers. As a result, the pair moves with such obvious poise and confidence that it wows the spectators.

Keeping your balance means respecting and valuing yourself as well as others and relying on your abilities, yet being able to ask for support when necessary. It has nothing to do with an "I don't need you" attitude, but rather your ability to stand on your own. Independence implies confidence, trust, and flexibility—the capacity to accept new conditions and quickly adapt to change. The ability to keep stable and stay attuned to your inner essence will help you make the right choices in the face of challenges and also resist temptations.

I regained my confidence and balance through Argentine tango. You should find your own way to transcend emotional blockages and let life itself flow freely through you. I highly recommend choosing something that involves a kinesthetic approach—utilizing your physical body. It can be yoga, playing music, volunteering, or participating in a sport. From painting to spiritual practice, the opportunities are endless.

Transformation and learning dramatically speed up when you involve both the body and mind. Think of children: They absorb the most amount of information at a very early age, when their bodies are flexible and in constant motion. Engaging your body will help you ingrain your new beliefs into your physiology. This, in turn, will help you move beyond cognitive understanding, where acting on your new convictions becomes natural. Employing your body is also invaluable for emotional release. Remember how I was able to overcome my fear of walking on fire by throwing myself into a tribal dance? The connection between your emotions and physiology is a two-way street. When you let go of old patterns of resentment, you may experience relief from chronic tensions in your muscles. The knots can dissolve, and pains disappear.

The exercise below will help you feel your core. It takes less than a minute, yet it can put you in a state of focus and determination, energize you, and inspire purpose-driven action. Try it now.

Feeling Your Core

Stand with your back and head straight, shoulders drawn back, yet relaxed. Feet are shoulder-width apart. Root your feet into the Earth, and make sure to breathe fully. Locate the spot just above your solar plexus, and imagine a string attached to it pulling your chest a bit upward into the sky. Feel the center of your body around your solar plexus and heart; sense the strength that comes from within. Feel the steady support of Mother Earth and allow the wisdom and intelligence of Father Sky to enter your body through the crown of your head. Let the confidence of being grounded and the guidance of divine perspective meet and intertwine in the center of your body. Expand this dual power and visualize it enveloping your entire being. Embrace and embody this strength and feel appreciation for it.

Did you experience an increase in your overall energy level? Do you feel more confident now? Imagine getting out of bed every morning and getting a hold of this power before you take your first step. Try it tomorrow morning.

Bring your steady core—emotional, physical, and mental balance—into relationships, yet remain flexible. Learn to connect with your essence and live from the strength within. This will attract a solid partner to you. Together you can gracefully dance through life and experience the bliss of connection, mutual understanding, care, and growth.

Step 6

Honor Yourself

ikki Willis met Nadia Salamanca when he was coming out of his first marriage and was re-discovering the freedom of single life. He felt an instant attraction and deep connection to Nadia, and they started dating. However, Mikki was determined not to be in a committed relationship. A handsome and successful filmmaker, Mikki had an array of women falling for him, and he wanted to keep his options open. He told Nadia about his intent and offered to have an open policy, where both of them could see other people. Even though Nadia deeply cared for Mikki and was falling in love with him, she lovingly told him that what he offered was not what she was looking for. She suggested that he do whatever he needed to get this urge out of his system and asked him not to call her while he was playing around. As a result, they went their separate ways.

Mikki was struck by Nadia's dignity. Unlike other women, she wasn't ready to give up her relationship vision and settle for less than she really desired just to hold on to him. Nadia wanted to share herself with Mikki when he was ready to receive her completely. While Mikki had a lot of fun meeting many beautiful women, his heart was yearning for Nadia. She, however, was gently declining his attempts to see her.

Nadia had to make the toughest decision and repeatedly say no to the man of her dreams. Yet, it was exactly her strength and unwavering self-respect that wowed Mikki and singled her out from all the other women he was meeting in glamorous Hollywood. As a result, Nadia's honoring of herself inspired Mikki to honor himself just the same. He decided to fully explore the part of his being that was drawn to this special woman. They got back together and completely devoted themselves to each other creating the most fascinating and inspiring relationship.

It's worth noting, however, that having dignity is vastly different from "playing hard to get." The latter pretentiously says, "I don't care for you," or "I am too busy," or "I am in high demand," in hopes of prompting the other person into an active pursuit. This chasing game is based on the psychology of "limited supplies" and, like other forms of manipulation, is incompatible with true intimacy and lasting happiness. True self-respect, on the other hand, denotes supreme honesty with oneself and a partner, where your integrity and your values remain uncompromised even for the sake of love.

Honoring yourself is not to be confused with arrogance or pride. These traits are products of deeply rooted and well-concealed insecurities. Superiority is simply an attempt of "little me" to feel more important and worthy of attention by putting others down. It is when we belittle ourselves and feel pitiful, or guilty, that we seek confidence by looking for flaws in people and despising them. Arrogance

I SAID, I'M IVY LEAGUE, A SURGEON, AND I DRIVE A PORSCHE. WHY AREN'T YOU NAKED YET?

is the opposite of self-respect, because true dignity results in humility and regarding others.

Valuing oneself is challenging for many people, because we are used to measuring worthiness based on appearance, performance, usefulness, or importance. However, once you look at yourself from a broader perspective of life as a whole, honoring yourself becomes a sacred cause. The non-physical *Source* energy morphs into various physical forms infinitely. In the tangible realm, however, we observe mortality and impermanence. This creates an illusion that a single organism is not that important. We even say that one's life can be significant or insignificant. Even the phrases used in our society, like "waste of life," represent this delusion. However, the term "waste" is exclusively a product of the human mind, because it does not exist in nature. Everything is utilized and recycled and contributes to the perpetuation of life and evolution. The tiniest creature, or even a molecule, has its purpose, and nothing is ever absolutely destroyed. Moreover, the importance and value of the eternal divine essence within every expression of life cannot be measured. It would be like trying to evaluate existence itself. You, as a unique expression of life and an extension of *Great Spirit*, are invaluable to the whole. Therefore, honoring yourself is nothing short of honoring the Creator, or God, or the Source of Life, whichever term you prefer.

In relationships, dignity is part of the foundation. If you don't respect yourself and your body, you will attract a partner who will reflect back your discourteous attitude toward yourself. On the other hand, your resolute integrity will speak for itself through your demeanor, and it won't be necessary to demand that others honor your values and principles. Eighty percent of our communication is non-verbal; people will sense your inner strength and decisiveness subconsciously.

Honoring yourself means wisely utilizing and cherishing your assets— your body, your mind, time, abilities, etc.—and gearing them toward your heartfelt purposes. It involves making choices that are consistent with the intelligence of your spirit. On the dance floor of your relationships, it prompts you to carefully select your partners and thoroughly execute every step of your dance.

Step 7

Create Space

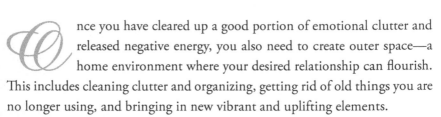

nce you have cleared up a good portion of emotional clutter and released negative energy, you also need to create outer space—a home environment where your desired relationship can flourish. This includes cleaning clutter and organizing, getting rid of old things you are no longer using, and bringing in new vibrant and uplifting elements.

Go through your closet and pull out everything you have not used in more than a year. Donate it or sell it to a recycled clothing store. Repeat the procedure with other areas of your household. Make sure you remove from visible display all pictures and sentiments reminding you of your former lovers. Replace them with the images related to your new relationship vision.

Examine your home for "partner compatibility." Is your place private and inviting for your lover to visit you? What mood does your interior design stimulate? Is it vibrant, relaxing, and luxurious, or gloomy, outdated, and depressing? Is your bed comfortable for two people? Is your bedroom alluring for lovemaking? How about the living room—is it suitable for a cozy evening at home with the *one*? If you were to buy a nice couch, wouldn't you first think about whether it would fit into your room? So, before you welcome a mate into your life, doesn't it make sense to make sure your environment is supportive of a relationship?

What about your schedule? Can it accommodate a romantic involvement? For many people, "I don't have time" is a legitimate-sounding excuse for unhappiness. Start dedicating time to your relationship now. Even before a partner appears in your life, devote time to learning, refining your beliefs, and practicing a chosen transformational medium such as sports, music, or the arts. Whatever activities you want to perform with your mate, start doing them on your own, and imagine how much fun it will be to share this experience with someone special.

Your communication circle is also important. If you have friends who constantly unload their problems on you or initiate pain-generating discussions, decrease the time you spend with them or set your interactions on a positive course. Get together more often with the people who stimulate you intellectually, emotionally, or spiritually, or the ones who are simply fun to be around. If you know couples who are happy together, hang out with them, and let their happiness rub off on you. Treasure yourself and your time; devote it to fulfilling and enjoyable encounters.

Foster confidence in bringing your relationship vision into reality. Notice affectionate pairs in public places, and praise them in your mind for finding each other. Any time you witness a healthy relationship, or hear or read about one, take it as a sign that you, too, are attracting personal happiness into your life.

Step 8

Follow
Your Heart

The heart has its reasons that reason knows nothing of...
It is the heart that feels God and not the reason.
—Blaise Pascal

Another secret I learned from my brilliant tango teachers is that every step in tango comes from the heart. In fact, the whole dance is an act of following one's heart. When you look at a tango couple embraced, you will see that their upper bodies are connected. Within their hearts is where the music is heard and inspiration is born. This is where the lead originates, and this is where the partner, who follows, receives the message.

We are multifaceted creatures armed with logical and analytical minds, complex emotional palettes, and powerful intuition. All of these are valuable tools, and each one of them performs an important function. Our ability to reason supports structure and helps us organize information. Our senses provide fullness and quality-of-life experience. Our intuition supplies a connection to *all*—visible and invisible, tangible and not yet materialized, to all times, and all possibilities. It is the gateway to the life itself and to its magnificent *Creator*.

Every so often, these elements are in disagreement, and while logic dictates one course of action, an emotional outburst leads the other way. Our minds can drive us crazy by constantly weighing out pros and cons, taking into consideration as much information as possible, and attempting to foresee all possible outcomes. Feelings can get out of control and lead to impulsive and irrational behaviors. And only *the truth in your heart is never loud, but this quiet voice holds all the wisdom you will ever need.*

In order to receive the divine guidance, which is always available, you have to quiet all mental noise, become an observer of your emotions, and feel the silence of your being. Then you will be able to hear the music and allow it to inspire you.

> *The secret of tango is in this moment of improvisation that happens between step and step. It is to make the impossible thing possible: to dance silence. This is essential to learn in tango dance, the real dance, that of the silence, of following the melody.*
> —Carlos Gavito, a legendary tango dancer

Seeing through the clarity of your heart allows you to *know* the pristine essence of your true nature and that of others. True freedom is discovered within, and the ultimate power is drawn from your heart's love and compassion. Allow this benevolent guidance to take you to the answers you are seeking, to peace, happiness, and to fulfilling your aspirations.

We connect to the *Divine Source* in the moments of inspiration. Any form of creativity expressed or perceived is a doorway to synchronicity with *Infinite Intelligence*. This is why we value art, because it speaks to our souls directly. This is why we lose our "self" in the creative process and gain the world in return. In other words, we dissolve the sense of separation—the ego—and become one with the divine genius, allowing it to flow into our art.

The essence of your being is the timeless life force that flows in and through you. It can be accessed whenever you like through prayer, meditation, or by being in nature. Also, you can learn to feel your very core—the heart of hearts, the wise infinite source within—using the meditative process below.

The Heart of Hearts Meditation

Find a quiet place, whether it be your favorite spot in nature, or in the coziness of your home. Get in a comfortable sitting position. Inhale deeply three times, and exhale slowly, each time focusing on relaxing your body. Then mentally count down from ten to one while releasing all tensions and thoughts with every exhale. For a while just sit with your eyes closed and focus on your breathing and your heartbeat. Ponder and *feel* the force, which makes you breathe and which beats your heart. If thoughts appear in your mind, just let them pass, giving them no attention at all, sort of observing them as if they were strangers, and focus instead on the life within you; relax into feeling it. Hear the *rhythm* of your breath and your heartbeat. Contemplate the rhythm of the ocean waves, the galloping of a horse and the rustling of leaves in the wind. Perceive your heartbeat and your breath to be part of the same rhythm of life that spins the Earth and galaxies.

Any high-speed movement and seeming craziness of daily life has stillness at its core. There is calmness in the depth of rapid waters, and even the devastating force of a hurricane holds tranquility in its eye. In your heart there is peacefulness also—reach for it. Feel the composure and certainty of your *soul*. It is intertwined with all of life, and it knows absolute well-being. Connect to the most reliable source of wisdom and knowledge within your heart. Know that you are loved and guided, appreciated, and adored. Enjoy the stillness, and see the light of your *spirit.* Contemplate its capacity. You are valuable beyond measure, as no one else can deliver your gifts to the world. Stay connected to your heart of hearts for as long as you like. To come out of this meditative state, in your mind count from one to five, and slowly open your eyes, regaining awareness of your surroundings.

At first, when you try this meditation, you may feel just glimpses of this connection, depending on how tense you are when you start. In time, you will be able to access your essence and operate from that place of wisdom within. This process is equally helpful in decision making or simply relaxing after an intense day.

Successful relationships require a similar intuitive approach. Your mind assumes the role of the ultimate protector (second best after your mother, of course) responsible for your safety. Consequently, it constantly runs a security check on the entire "outside" world, including people. It drives you toward comfort and certainty, but not necessarily happiness. In order to open your heart, you need to quiet your mind. Remember, a successful relationship means growth, which cannot happen when your defense mechanisms are activated.

When meeting a new partner, how do you find clarity among mental chatter, emotional excitement, and the hormonal surge of a new attraction? Balance these forces by connecting to the source within. Listen to your mind, trust your heart, and follow your intuition.

As a woman, when truly coming from your heart, your primary focus cannot be on what your potential partner does for a living, how much he makes, or what kind of car he drives. Your heart will look for a courageous spirit who offers his deep love and guidance to you, whom you can trust and to whom you can surrender. The importance of his outer attributes fades. You will be attracted to his confidence, power, passion, and open heart. You will be moved by his genuineness and boldness, not by the size of his penis or house.

As a man, guided by the wisdom in your heart, you cannot be solely focused on model-like appearances. You will seek inspiration, radiance, devotion, and a free-flowing offering of love. You will be drawn to the fire in her eyes and grace in her movement, to a mysterious note in her smile and the sound of her voice. You will be mesmerized by her feminine glow, not by the size of her silicone breasts or culinary abilities.

It is perfectly normal to look for physical attraction and chemistry and to take into consideration domestic aspects. However, when a union is based on intellectual, sexual, and household compatibility alone, it lacks the vital foundation for long-term success. Looks change as we age; sexual passion unsupported by deep soulful connection fades, and economic and life situations may become unfavorable. What is left then? Without deep caring, appreciation, and love for each other, a relationship is not sustainable.

Your heart is looking for real treasures. If you follow its guidance, your findings will always exceed your best expectations. All aspects of your mate, including external, will be pleasing to you. In fact, confident men who are driven by a higher purpose are typically successful and capable of providing for their family. Women who bloom in their hearts are perceived as beautiful.

Step 9

Be Authentic

*To be yourself in a world that is constantly trying to
make you something else is the greatest accomplishment.*
—Ralph Waldo Emerson

hy do we value original art over almost identical forgery? Why
does authentic Louis Vuitton cost thousands, while imitations
are cheap? Why are new ideas and inventions highly regarded?
We innately appreciate the creative process an artist, designer, or engineer
goes through to deliver his masterpiece. We consider genius the ability to
ride a wave of inspiration and to connect to the *Divine Source* for guidance,
and to enrich the world as a result. We praise the courage to escape from the
conventional framework.

In personal lives, however, we often try to blend with others and remain
within the "norm." We mold our looks, behaviors, and responses to match
socially accepted standards. We restrain our unique edge and measure our

own adequacy, abilities, and self-worth against those of others. As a result, we don't even know who we are. Instead of proclaiming our individuality through our demeanor, character, and deeds, we derive our sense of self from the opinions of others. Rather than declaring our identity, we receive one.

In true intimacy all masks and pretenses are removed, and our bare soul becomes exposed. Hiding your real nature becomes impossible in the long run. Therefore, revealing your own face and sincere behavior becomes a necessity and should be practiced before you meet the *one*.

The level of vulnerability and openness you experience in an intimate relationship is both extremely terrifying and exceptionally liberating. A heart-to-heart connection requires unsurpassed honesty with yourself and with your partner, the ability to face—and, if necessary, share—your fears, and then to step beyond them. It is a path of uncertainty and humbleness—an "all in" game.

It is no wonder that so many prefer floating on the surface to diving deep. Hundreds of Facebook "friends," via text message conversations, virtual sex on the islands of *Second Life*[9], and phony chitchats at live parties became our safe havens for communication. While undoubtedly comforting, versatile, and entertaining, they take our time and serve as a distraction from actual reality. We get addicted to the constant information feed, and it excuses us from the necessity to think or feel deeply, because we are busy consuming. It becomes quantity versus quality; it inflates our outer shell and leaves us empty and unfulfilled inside. An intimate relationship requires depth, and perishes if approached superficially.

The main enemy of honesty is the fear of rejection. All we want is love. We often pretend, exaggerate, or lie because we are afraid that we are not worthy to be loved for who we are. So we put on makeup, padded bras, and undergo painful procedures to become more desirable. We brag about our careers or try to impress others with our intellect, sense of humor, or anything else we think people might find appealing. All of this would be fine if these behaviors weren't often driven by deeply rooted insecurities and the fear of being not enough.

---

9   Online virtual world, where users participate as avatars

Trying to entice a romantic partner through a glittery affectation is like selling a product for the wrapping. You might succeed, but your lover will be attracted to your facade. This means you will have to keep it on at all times and constantly maintain it and prevent fading and aging, which will happen sooner or later anyway. If you dare to reveal what's inside the fancy covering, you might risk hearing that you have changed and are no longer the same person your mate was enchanted by.

WELL, OBVIOUSLY I NEED TO GO BIGGER, BECAUSE I'M STILL ATTRACTING JERKS.

In a fairy tale, why does the Beauty have to fall in love with the Beast before his real appearance of a handsome prince is revealed? This story teaches that true love sees beyond impressive appearance. It has no mercantile motives and is based on sincere care for another.

A great relationship inspires authenticity. As a result, such a union becomes a source of exhilarating freedom for both partners. It is a real blessing to feel genuinely adored for being who you are. Know that the *one* for you will embrace you completely and love you unequivocally. What some people may have considered as your character "flaws," he will find amusing. What you thought of as imperfection in your body, he will kiss and perceive as beautiful. Whatever you deemed as your limitation, he will show you as your strength; if there was insecurity, he will teach you how to draw confidence from it.

Once I was on my way to attend a conference in Las Vegas. The passengers were boarding the airplane and getting situated. All of a sudden the busy traveling crowd got noisier, as one couple drew everyone's attention. A glowing woman was carrying a wedding gown from David's Bridal. Almost every passenger turned to cheer them on.

It so happened that the groom-to-be sat right next to me, and his bride had a seat elsewhere. Naturally, I turned to him and said "Congratulations!" His "thank you" was rather dry. I could tell he was nervous about the whole thing. I decided to mind my own business and go back to reading a book. When we landed, an older gentleman from the aisle seat next to us congratulated my neighbor again. This time the guy said, "Thank you! It's a rather frightening experience." I asked him why he said that. He replied, "Well, it used to be my way, and now it's gonna be her way." The gentlemen from the aisle seat counseled, "Just say, 'Yes, dear,' and you will be okay." I could not keep quiet.

"No! She respects you for your ways, doesn't she?" A glee lit the groom's face. "Yes."

"So, you should keep your ways! The greatest gift you can give her is to be who you are. She loves you for who you are! Don't change it!" He smiled and thanked me, and we parted ways.

In a great relationship, you don't morph into someone you are not, just to keep your partner happy. To the contrary, your mate *knows* your true nature and continuously calls it to surface. You are not expected to always agree with one another. It is from your disagreements that new ideas are born and mutual growth is stimulated.

Each one of us comes into this world to make an exclusive contribution. Authenticity is free-flowing self-expression. Imagine your inner essence, talents, and natural way of being as a body of water. When restrained by boundaries and without movement, it stagnates and rots. When it flows freely, it cleanses itself along the way, replenishes its minerals, washes off the obstacles, and shapes its stream organically within the landscape. Your exquisiteness is revealed in the same gracious movement when you follow your inspirations, speak your mind, and dare to make a statement.

When you and your mate are authentic, you never cease to surprise one another and constantly notice new facets in each other's personalities. Together you discover new ways to have fun and enjoy life ever more. In such a relationship your daily "routine" consists of playful interactions, sparked creativity, intellectual stimuli, and passionate romantic moments.

You don't need to be perfect—there is no such thing! Yet, you would want to bring your best to a relationship, because this is your contribution. This means being your authentic congruent self: aligned to the power within and to the wisdom in your heart, free-spirited, and joyous. You owe it to yourself and to your beloved. This authenticity is extremely charming in people and is a gem of a find.

Step 10

Accept Your Partner

When dreaming about a romantic relationship, we create an ideal in our minds. Naturally, we include only the things we consider to be good, into the picture. However, the actual experience is never one-sided. The *one* you were longing for is not an image retouched to perfection from the magazine page. She is not an ever-young seductress with a short memory, who acts like a lady and never complains. He is not a mind reader for your wishes, who spends his days planning surprises for you and never stops delivering coffee to you in bed and showering you with flowers and gifts.

The love of your life is a real person, with moods and quirks, wrinkles and moles, ups and downs. He will never do everything in the way you consider to be right. And she will never become completely rational.

Somehow our society got infected with the dangerous and entirely bogus idea that we can change another person. People invest years of their lives in useless attempts to re-shape their mate into an ideal they once came up with. This is futile, and it never works. Others test their influence over people in order to boost their significance and to feel powerful.

You can never change anyone, but you can inspire and uplift that person. Moreover, wanting to modify somebody implies believing that there is something wrong with him in the first place. When you have a diminishing perception of a person, you can never fully appreciate him or evoke his best

HE'S WONDERFUL. IT'LL ALMOST BE A PITY WHEN WE GET MARRIED AND I HAVE TO CHANGE EVERYTHING ABOUT HIM.

qualities. It's like reading bad reviews about a restaurant and then going there hoping to enjoy dinner by giving instructions to the chef and to the waitress, and explaining to the owner how to run his business.

Your lover does not need to be saved or straightened out. Your opinion regarding things and people and how they should be is only one of many points of view and cannot be claimed as absolute truth. Respecting your partner, his own journey, his values, and perspectives is the cornerstone of a healthy relationship.

Besides, imagine if you and your mate were always in agreement. What if you shared the same outlook in life, approached problems in the same way, and offered identical solutions? You would have matching preferences and similar habits, and would always only please each other. Can you picture this scenario? You would both howl of boredom! It would be like eating sweet cake all day every day. Too much sugar would make you sick.

A relationship needs to be exciting and interesting. Therefore, you and your mate should challenge each other and grow together. You will spice it up with occasional disagreements and even a heated argument, bringing in unexpected flavors and unusual behaviors.

When you love someone at her worst, you surely will love her at her best. At times we all feel out of whack and get off balance, which often causes hostile behavior. The kindest person can be rude, and the most tactful

disapproval. Complete acceptance is essential for being able to open up and be totally honest. Receive the *one* graciously, and offer him the gift of non-judgment.

Your function in a relationship is to reflect back to your mate the beauty of his soul, the grace and power of his spirit, and the unique preciousness of his heart. The admiration in your eyes will tell him all of that. Your devoted love is an inspiration for your mate to be at his best.

Make Every Date Great!

*In order to find a lifetime of happiness
you have to find happiness in the moment.*
—Aleksey Vays

Now it's time to get on the dance floor and practice your steps! You will probably have to tango with a few partners and polish your moves before the *one* knocks your socks off. In order for every dance to be enjoyable, you must select your partner carefully. The other important ingredients are your attitude and your mood. Intend to have fun and enjoy the dance.

Dating can be disappointing and discouraging until you adopt a mindset that will make every date great. I used to experience a mini-heartbreak every time I went out and realized he was not the *one*. I felt disappointed, discouraged, and a bit irritated. My confidence in finding the love of my life was fading.

My dating experience transformed when I switched my agenda from finding a life partner, to enjoying the time with the wonderful men who came into my experience. I started receiving every new admirer as a gift. I stopped taking for granted the fact that they were attracted to me and began appreciating it. I focused more on nice things they did versus something they failed to do. I was on a hunt to find the best qualities in each person I went out with. Noticing and appreciating these traits increased my genuine respect for my dates and prospects and made interactions more enjoyable. Parting ways became more artful and hardly caused sorrows anymore.

Treating dating as an exploration and adventure made it into a whole new game. Habitual Q & A sessions and going over the "checklist" converted into lighthearted and fun conversations. I stopped quizzing men and responded to their "serious" questions with jokes. It was no longer about "what you do," "what you like," "where you're from," or "Do you want to have children?" but rather about two people savoring unique time together and enjoying each other's company.

What a relief it was. Having zero expectations will set you free. I did not go out looking for a husband anymore. I opened my heart and my mind to whatever experiences came my way. This does not mean that I dropped my values or was ready to settle for just anything—quite the contrary. However, I did not attempt to control the dance floor any longer. I was not showing up to have the ultimate dance. I wanted to have the best dance possible at that moment in time.

You do not dance to settle; you dance because the music inspires you and you cannot stand still, because your partner's eyes sparkle and call you for adventure. You feel enthused and want to paint a melody with your feet. As long as you continue to flow on the dance floor, more inspirations, more passion, more bliss, and more oneness will await you. Open up to the possibilities, and embrace every unexpected note in a song and in every new move your partner offers.

When you collected the images for your vision board, you did not feel much disappointment over those pictures that didn't fit your purpose. You flipped through a magazine, selected suitable photos, and simply discarded the rest. If some article was too long and took up too many pages, you didn't get upset. You also didn't care much if there was nothing to your liking in a particular publication. You just moved on. Treat your dating the same way. Focus on the best characteristics of the person you are with, and add them to the mental image of your desired mate. Omit whatever displeases you.

For instance, you might not feel chemistry with your date, which would mean that you are not a good match, but you might love his sense of humor and share a few great laughs. Instead of complaining in your mind that he is not the *one*, appreciate the fun that you are having, and wish for you and your chosen partner to laugh just as easily. Also, add the experiences to your relationship vision. If you like the restaurant you are in, imagine visiting the same place later with the love of your life.

Practice being authentic, and speak the truth, even when you are tempted to do otherwise. If someone disapproves of you, let it be her problem, not yours. When a prominent American financier and presidential advisor Bernard Baruch was asked how he handled seating arrangements for his dinner parties, he replied, "I never bother about that. Those who mind don't matter, and those who matter, don't mind." You can never please everybody anyway. As long as you give your best, respect others, and value yourself, there will be people who genuinely appreciate you.

Once you fully integrate with your true identity—your authentic self, expand your horizons by replacing limiting beliefs, and open your heart, the congruent partner will show up.

Do Not Look, and You Shall Find

he secret to finding the *one* is in releasing the urge to search. Have you ever lost your keys or something else that you desperately needed in the moment? You went around in circles and couldn't find it, only to discover later that it was right there in front of you, and you failed to see it. Looking for a life partner is the same tricky process. While you are seeking, you cannot find her. It is precisely the moment you give up or expect nothing special to happen that somebody touches your heart and turns your world around.

Why is it that love often comes unexpectedly and doesn't call in advance to announce its arrival? If it did, you would set your expectations and prepare accordingly. You would wear your hottest attire, put a charming smile on your face, and you would keep a few proven jokes up your sleeve. You would eagerly anticipate the appearance of the ideal you pictured in your mind. When the real person showed up at your door, you would measure him up against the dream version you envisioned. Then you would meticulously take notice of every mismatch and cast him off as unsuitable, or even worse, try to change him into the person you had in mind.

Dianne Collins shared a wise insight regarding the attitude of non-attachment to a result. She said that if you are looking to connect with a person, understand that your relationship will unfold like a flower blossom. It will take a certain amount of attention, nourishing, water, and light, but you don't have to push the bud to become a beautiful orchid. Dianne also advised to be aware that everything has its own life cycle. Some relationships are meant to be short-term, some are meant for longer duration, and others are meant for a lifetime. Not clinging to an outcome will allow you to develop profound connections naturally.

Expectations are very particular and rigid by nature and hold a strong possibility of not being met. Consequently, they introduce the fear of disappointment into the equation. This fear triggers the protection mode, and your heart closes off. True love cannot find its way to you, because you are not open to receive.

Love is generous, kind, and accepting. It thrives in open and unguarded hearts and shines its light unconditionally. It reaches out to everyone, but is welcomed and seen only by those people who have the courage to be vulnerable. Love's treasures are revealed to those who embrace its pulsating and flowing nature, understand that it transforms, molds, and evolves, and to those who dare to feel deeply and value freedom over security. *Love is gracious, and it puts everyone on the same pedestal, so your ego cannot look down on anyone.*

To find love, your state of being has to be pure: relaxed, natural, joyous, and appreciative. You have to already be in love—with life, people, yourself, that pretty cloud in the sky, and the playful bird on your balcony, or the silly driver in the car next to you who sings out loud. Put down your protective armor and give your kindness and affection to everyone you can. Do not discriminate with who you believe deserves your love. Withholding your soul's gifts is painful to you, first and foremost. Just like rain doesn't choose which plant is worthy of receiving water and showers onto everything liberally, your true nature calls for sheer giving without reservations.

Keep your mind and your heart open. Share your warmth generously and trade expectations for new inspirations. Know most definitely that there is another loving heart yearning for yours, and one day you will inevitably find each other.

The Home
of Love

Where does love come from, and where does it live? To answer this question, I will share the story told by Amber Hartnell, with her gracious permission.

"I was two when my parents divorced, and I was seven when my mother passed away. The night that she died she visited me in spirit. She planted a seed within me, which was a tremendous gift and influenced my entire life. When she was saying goodbye to me that night, she said that the time coming up was going to be extremely difficult, but absolutely necessary. Yet, I was going to get through it, and I would always be loved. So, there was knowing activated within me that challenges are okay and that there is always a purpose within them, and if I focus on the purpose, I will always find it. It's like focusing on a pearl that you know is in a clam of an oyster, so you can crack through a shell and discover the treasure at its center.

"For the next seven years, I went to live with my father, who was an alcoholic, physically abusive, and had a very angry wife. I lived in a kind of a classic *Cinderella* story. I had to take care of the entire family from the age of seven to fourteen. It was extremely difficult, and yet I always had this sense of a light at the end of the tunnel, knowing that this was on purpose. The amazing thing was, no matter how abhorrent my stepmother and my dad were to me, I always felt love for them, unshakable.

"I was not getting love from anywhere on the outside, but I always felt love. This showed me at an early age that it doesn't come from another person—love is what we are. We can choose to allow it, no matter what is going on around us, and we are a generator of it."

It is silly to look for love, because it is not outside of you, but within the treasury of your heart. This is why it is easy, natural, and always available. Each one of us is a source of love, yet we persistently look for it to come from others. Often, we are like a water fountain that is thirsty. No one can ever satisfy your yearning, until you acknowledge your own nature and fulfill your purpose of an affluent, vivifying source. The more love you give, the more it flows from you.

Your lover simply helps you to open your heart, and his eyes looking at you with admiration merely reflect the beauty of your own soul. Your beloved will echo to you where you're impeding the flow of love and where you set the boundaries on acceptance. You will challenge each other to expand your capacity to love beyond confinements. The degree of your openness and vulnerability will keep increasing, which in turn will grow your ability to experience joy, freedom, and ecstasy of life.

It is an exhilarating ride into unknown territory; this is why it seems frightening. However, it pushes the gates to the Kingdom of Happiness wide open. *In reality, when you allow yourself to truly love, you cannot be hurt.* The feelings of affection and care toward another are delightful on their own. We feel pain when our expectations are not met or when our urges are not satisfied. Love, on the other hand, is self-sufficient. When you love, you need nothing in return. Because you are overjoyed and overflowing with grace, you want to give and shine your light onto others. Nurture your home of Love—your heart— and share its warmth benevolently, for you have an unlimited supply.

Magic Moment

Shared by Dianne and Alan Collins:

"A few years back, we spontaneously decided to drive from London to Paris for a weekend. This was in August, which is the vacation month in France, and our attempts to find a hotel without an advanced reservation were miserably failing. We went from one place to another only to hear the same answer that everything is booked.

"So we set a powerful intent to find a fabulous place to stay and to enjoy Paris to the fullest, yet we had no idea how it would come about. It was getting late, but we kept walking around searching for accommodations.

"Finally, we walked into a beautiful hotel. Both of us decided that this was the place where our prayers would be answered. However, a lengthy conversation with a receptionist yielded the same response—no rooms were available. Nonetheless, this did not shake our determination and focus. We didn't allow disappointment to creep in and kept trusting in the positive outcome. We stepped outside and saw a man cleaning a window. He turned to us and asked, "Are you looking for a place to stay?" We looked at each other and said in unison, "Yes!" It turned out that he was asked to manage and rent an apartment while its owners were out of town.

"Our "earth angel" guided us through the door and down short hallways to a tiny elevator that took us right into the living area of an amazing studio, straight out of the pages of *Architectural Digest*. It was meticulous, clean, and minimalism at its best. The vibrant color of the sleek red sofa blended perfectly with the mirror-surfaced marble floor, checkered white, red, and black. The windows on the far wall allowed in bright light and looked out over the village street below, where we could watch passersby chattering away, enjoying the balmy summer evening. The kitchen was tiny, yet everything was at our fingertips, functional, and all of it hi-tech, including the espresso machine. The most memorable and amazing room, however, was the bathroom. The

Recognize the One for You

I remember asking my mom when I was little, "How do I know when I love someone?" She said, "Well, when it happens, you'll know," and her answer still kept my question open. When I probed for more details, she always brought up mutual respect, saying that it is one of the most important ingredients. My mom and dad have been happily married for over thirty-seven years, but unfortunately she had no better way of explaining to me what she felt in her heart.

As a result, I grew up and started kissing frogs, hoping that one of them would magically turn into a handsome prince and take my breath away. When this strategy didn't work, I focused on meeting a prince who would look and act like one without the need for magic transformation. It turned out that fairy tale-like princes are extinct as a species. Finally, instead of chasing fictional characters, I began seeking something timeless and of real value—deep connection and true caring.

Once you know what you are after, it becomes much easier to find. If you have practiced the pervious steps, your intuition should be finely tuned, and you should be open to receive what you have asked for. Recognizing the love of your life will be really easy for you.

My husband and I had each developed a clear relationship vision long before we met. In my case, I had been confused for so long that I had come to doubt my own ability to identify the right person. So I asked the Universe or the *Divine Source*—whatever you like to call it—for my man to know right away that I am his chosen woman. I wanted him to be one hundred percent confident and convince me, should I be in doubt. Aleksey, on the other hand, had always understood that he would immediately recognize her when he met the girl of his dreams. And this is exactly what happened. He knew instantly and convinced me (rather quickly).

I asked Aleksey how he knew right away that I was the *one* for him. He said that throughout his dating life there were two voices speaking in his head. One of them was always skeptical, asking, "How long is this one gonna last? You know she is not the *one*, you are just wasting your time," and the other one was saying, "We are just having fun." He says that when he met me, both of these voices were suddenly quiet. There was *knowing* and no inner dialogue. Also, the moment he looked into my eyes, he saw—he sensed—our future life together.

I have interviewed many couples and asked them to share the story of how they met. Remarkably, while the details and locations of each rendezvous were unique, the essence of the overall experience was the same. To give you a better sense of what to anticipate, below are some typical circumstances that occur when you meet the *one*:

- It often happens when you least expect it
- It happens naturally and organically
- You feel relaxed, confident, and at ease
- Even if you don't fall in love right away, you genuinely like this person
- Your communication is effortless

Rather often, there are also some mystical indicators or signs that confirm your subconscious suspicion that the person you just met is the *one* for you. For instance, the day after Aleksey and I met, he volunteered to take me to the airport. I was not in love with him yet, but my heart was opening up to his sincere intent and amazing persistence. We were parting ways at the first security check, when an awkward moment occurred—I wasn't sure if I should kiss him on the cheek or just give him a hug. I took the safe route, and we hugged. Then I walked up to the woman who was to check my ID and boarding pass. To my utter surprise, she said, "Oh, come on! Go back and give him a real kiss! And make it count this time." Stunned, I compliantly turned around and went back. He gave me one more memorable hug and I gently kissed his cheek. There were no other passengers or airport staff around. Just the three of us: Aleksey, me, and the Angel in the uniform.

Peggy McColl shared another incredible story about meeting her husband, Denis. Peggy was divorced and single for a few years. She built a successful career working from home and was happy with her life. However, she reached a point where she wanted to share her experiences with someone special. She set up a clear intent and wrote the description of her mate and of their future relationship, trusting the Universe to handle the "how" part. Since she made no effort to meet someone, her caring friends started offering various ideas from online dating to going out to meet people. Peggy, however, gently declined their offers. They nagged, "What do you think—he is just going to show up at your door?" "Well, maybe," she replied and continued to live as before.

One day she was walking her dog around the neighborhood. She noticed a guy who was moving into a house nearby. He was unpacking and walking back and forth unloading the truck. Peggy's dog noticed another shih tzu, which was tied up at the front of the house. Peggy followed her four-legged friend to the front lawn. Denis noticed her and came up to say hi. The instant she saw this masculine man, a thought crossed her mind: "This is the kind of guy I want to have in my life." As they casually chatted, she really liked his personality and his nature.

The right partner will truly appreciate and accept you completely. Your insecurities will fade in the presence of your beloved, because you will be received, embraced, and loved wholly. Your limitations will dissolve, as your mate will encourage and support you all the way.

For Mikki Willis it became clear that Nadia was the girl of his dreams after one incident when he took her on a motorcycle ride. They arrived at an intersection with a four-way signal. Across them was another biker—a man about sixty or seventy years old, with a long gray beard, and a younger lady was sitting behind him. Mikki is ten years older than Nadia. Some insecure thoughts crept into his mind, like, "I wonder how our age difference will play out. What if I start showing my age and Nadia doesn't?" So, he jokingly said to Nadia, while pointing to the other couple, "That's what you have to look forward to in a few years." Nadia squeezed him tight, and with genuine excitement said, "Awesome!" Mikki couldn't see her face, as she was sitting behind him, but he could feel her sincerity. It stunned Mikki how deeply Nadia cared and how much she was in love with the essence of who he was, not only with the outer attributes. Such acceptance gave him tremendous freedom to be authentic, without pretending or trying to keep any image. To this day they often encourage each other by saying, "Stop hiding! Go for it!" inspiring one another to grow and reach for bigger goals.

Another intricate element about recognizing the right mate is very primal and rarely talked about. It's the natural body scent. If you are a good match with your mate, you will love the scent of your partner's skin. It will seem better than any perfume to you. Our bodies are very intelligent and supply plenty of instinctive responses, which can be used as guidance.

If you are an auditory person, the tone of your beloved's voice will sound like music to your ears. If your visual perceptions are highly developed, you will find the appearance of your mate aesthetically pleasing. If you are predominantly kinesthetic, your lover will evoke delightful sensations in you. *You will be attracted and strongly drawn to the right partner; however, you will not be overwhelmed with lust to the point of losing control.* Your mutual magnetism will be powerful, yet graceful and conscious. You will be on the same wavelength, and your connection will develop swiftly and harmoniously. The *one* will inspire you to behave naturally, and the circumstances around you will fall organically into place.

Eden: How I Met the One

A leksey and I met in an idyllic spot aptly named Eden, located on the outskirts of the Sonoran Desert in Arizona. I had come with my friends to enjoy the hot springs and to take a break from my busy schedule in Los Angeles. Eden's rustic environment is informal, and that morning my look was vastly different from my usual city makeup, high heels, and designer clothes. I was walking to take a dip in the pool. My hair was loosely tied in a bun, I wore flip-flops and a robe, and a towel draped around my neck.

On my way, I met a friendly guy with a chess set in his hands. He introduced himself and asked if I knew how to play. In fact, I loved playing chess, but I had not practiced for years and didn't think I could be a challenging enough partner. So, I advised him to find my other friend Vassily, who was more skilled as a player.

I was in a small pool with my girlfriend, when Aleksey walked by again. He inquired once more about the game. This time I agreed. Soon my friend left, and we began playing. In the middle of the game, sunlight lit my face,

150

and Aleksey looked deeply into my eyes. He said, "Oh, God! Those eyes…" That was the moment he fell in love with me, and I sensed it, too, on some level. I looked back into his eyes and smiled. I thought to myself, "Your eyes are pretty, too," but I didn't voice it. However, as I discovered later, he knew exactly what I thought and literally read my mind.

He won the game, and I was ready to go on with my day. Aleksey asked about my plans and offered to keep me company. For the rest of the day, he was glued to me. I did not mind, because his attention was discreet and flattering. He was fun to be around, really nice, and remarkably sincere and straightforward, which was very refreshing compared to the often-pretentious LA crowd.

In the evening a large group of people gathered by the Big Pool. This is the largest pool in Eden. Rumor has it that in the beginning of the last century it was the biggest pool in the entire Western US. Bright stars dotted the endless sky. Cool air caused the pool's warm spring water to evaporate, creating a mystical haze over its surface.

Somebody brought an audio player, and Thievery Corporation, followed by Enigma, put finishing touches on the allure of the night. The music inspired a group of five or six women, who grabbed glow sticks from the edge of the pool and went in about waist-deep. They started dancing in unison as if they had practiced for months. Their enchanting improvisation was breathtaking and left us and other spectators completely mesmerized.

When the music and the dance ended, Aleksey and I swam to the far end of the pool. Night birds were singing on the trees around us. The water was reflecting the light of thousands of stars. The magic in the air was almost tangible. It was just the two of us. Aleksey told me that he was in love with me. I said that love is a treasurable feeling to have in one's heart. Then I added that I did not see much future for the two of us, because there were miles between us, as we lived in different states, and there were many other complications. His response was amazingly wise and simple. He said that if the feelings are real, then none of these things can be considered obstacles.

The next morning he had to drive back to Tucson, and I was returning to Phoenix with my friends and from there flying back to Los Angeles. Aleksey insisted he take me to the airport. Knowing that my girlfriend would be relieved if she didn't have to drive me, I agreed. Aleksey and I parted ways with the understanding that he would see me later in the afternoon before my flight. He gave me the most remarkable and sincere hug of my life. He held me tight, yet gently, as if I were the most precious possession ever. I felt his deep caring and his heart pounding hard ready to jump out of his chest. He left.

At first my girlfriend welcomed the news about Aleksey taking me to the airport; then she suddenly asked, "But doesn't he live in Tucson?"

"Yes," I said.

"Are you crazy? It's a two-hour drive for him each way! You are torturing this guy, and you are not even serious about him!"

I was shocked. Since I didn't live in Arizona, I assumed Tucson was a Phoenix suburb. I had no idea it was like going from San Diego to Los Angeles. I called him immediately to cancel the arrangement. But Aleksey would not let me off the hook. He assured me that it would be his pleasure and still insisted. I gave in.

On the way to the airport, he audaciously, but tactfully, suggested I invite him to visit me in Los Angeles. Once again I was speechless. I agreed, hoping to get out of it later. Needless to say, he did not take no for an answer. He negated all of my reasonable attempts to postpone his visit. Over the phone I told him not to expect much if he comes, that he will be sleeping on the floor in the living room and that I don't cook (even though I am an excellent cook and I love it). Aleksey agreed to all the restrictions and flew to LA the very next weekend. When he e-mailed me his flight info, he informed me that there was limited availability for return tickets and he will be staying three nights instead of two, hoping that I wouldn't mind. His boldness kept startling me, but at the same time, he was super nice and sincere, so I couldn't even get mad at him.

I was secretly curious how he would move forward from there. I thought I would keep him at a distance and he would get intimidated by me. I was friendly, but expressed zero romantic interest…at least that's what I thought I did. However, he was unwavering and completely ignored my little plan. On the evening of his arrival we went to my favorite sushi place in Beverly Hills for dinner and then decided to take a walk in the neighborhood. As we strolled down Rodeo Drive, a strong fragrance of growing petunias caught our attention. We walked by large flowerpots overflowing with purple and white blooms hanging on poles along the street. Aleksey suggested we get closer to smell them. The moment I reached for the flower heads, he reached for my face and kissed me. He caught me by surprise again, and I didn't resist. My intent to remain friends was carried away with the light spring breeze of the night. By the time he had to go back to Tucson, he managed to open my heart, and I fell for him.

When apart, we talked on the phone every day for hours and exchanged the most beautiful e-mails with poetry, and we both looked forward to our next rendezvous. In two weeks he drove to LA, and we spent another weekend together.

The first time he asked me to marry him was three weeks after we met. Yes, he had to ask three times. It was not a formal proposal; actually none of the three were traditional. We were in my kitchen kissing, and he asked if I'd marry him. I said, "Maybe." Persistent as he is, Aleksey asked me again the very next day on the beach. This time my response was "definitely maybe." The last time he proposed a few weeks later, when I was visiting him in Tucson. He didn't really ask me to marry him anymore. He painted a vivid vision of our life together, and invited me to be part of it, and it was irresistible. Our daily life as a couple is even better than that dream which compelled me. It is filled with Magic Moments, stimulating challenges, and fun adventures.

If you are curious, go to www.BestThingEver.com. You can see some photos of Eden.

Magic Moment

We were driving late at night and decided to stop at a gas station. Aleksey wanted to get a snack, and I went to use the bathroom. When I returned, he was already in the car. I asked him what he got, and he showed me ice cream. "Did you need anything?" he inquired. "Not really, but I was kinda hoping for M&Ms," I said. He pulled a pack of M&Ms out of his pocket and handed them to me. "I got these for you." I smiled and kissed him in appreciation.

It was so heartwarming and amazing! He literally read my mind, because it is unusual for me to get something at a gas station, and I don't typically eat popular candies and snacks.

PART VII

Commitment

The Essence of Your Promise

leksey and I were on a plane headed to Argentina, where we were planning to spend some time with my parents and celebrate winter holidays. The American Airlines flight crew was very friendly and took good care of us. We started chatting with a flight attendant—a charming middle-aged woman with a warm smile and sweet demeanor. In the conversation she recalled a couple from her church that wanted to renew their vows after only a year of being married. She considered it so touching and wise for the long-term marriage success. Then she asked us, "Are you guys going to renew your wedding vows?" As soon as we both enthusiastically nodded, she said, "How often will you do that?" We laughed, and I said, "We renew our vows every moment of every day." The whole section of passengers around us cheered us on. Our approach to commitment is vastly different from the existing convention, and our mutual devotion is declared continually, instead of being a one-time vow.

Commitment is a controversial subject. It is considered a vital ingredient in a healthy relationship. It demonstrates the partners' loyalty to each other

I'M IN, I'M TOTALLY IN, I JUST NEED A LEEETLE MORE TIME TO SEE WHAT ELSE IS OUT THERE.

and is perceived as a guarantee for long-term success. On the other hand, commitment seems frightening for many reasons. For most people, pledging monogamy and making a promise to the chosen partner for a lifetime is a big step to take. This implies waving all opportunities to pursue other people and sticking together through any and all circumstances. In traditional understanding, it calls for the waiving of some personal freedoms and offers a vague promise of the "happily ever after" in return.

Even the prominent clinical psychologist Katherine Woodward Thomas calls love an "utterly steadfast", or "undeniably fixed and invariable promise."[11] While I respect this author greatly, I think that this very approach is what scares people, because it imprisons a person by his own promise. This attitude is also responsible for many people remaining in unhappy marriages, because we don't want to break our "invariable promise" and be perceived as a "bad" or "flaky" person who gives up.

Think of your love and your mate as a beautiful bird that came to live in your garden. It entertains you with pleasing songs throughout the day; you are mesmerized by its graceful soaring in the skies above and cute mannerisms when it prinks. It starts trusting you and lets you touch it and eats off your hands. This bird becomes so dear to your heart that you are terrified at the thought it might leave you one day. You decide to assure this bird's presence in your life, so you catch it, clip its wings, and put it in a cage.

---

11   Katherine Woodward Thomas *Calling in "The One"* Three Rivers Press, 2004

Your guests are wowed by a unique living trophy you now own. You feel certain and secure, because the bird cannot leave you and everyone around you is informed that it is yours. However, the bird stops singing, its feathers lose its sleekness and glow, and you cannot witness the glorious flight any longer. It pecks you when you try to pet it and refuses to take food from your hands. You are disappointed—this is not the bird you cherished so much. Encaged, it lost its charm.

We attempt to extract commitment from another to serve as a security seal—a proof of ownership. Next, we place unreasonable restrictions on this person, demanding our mate's exclusive attention and taking offense when he even notices other attractive people. By loving someone you don't become blind; you still notice beauty in the world and appreciate it even more than before. Why restrict your partner? You cannot request of the sun that it shine on you exclusively; that is asking the impossible. Whether your partner appreciates a flower, a nice car, or an attractive human being is irrelevant. We do not possess our partners, we share the journey with them, and we should not expect to train another like a dog and keep him on a short leash. Even if you succeed, your partner has now lost self-respect, and you will eventually lose respect for your partner, too.

The customs of our society contradict the very nature of love as a free-flowing, gracious offering. Love is a gift, not a payment on an obligation. No wonder why many people instinctively resist the rigid and obligatory approach to a relationship.

On the other hand, isn't commitment the cornerstone of any achievement? Isn't it necessary in order to keep a steady course and not waver in the face of adversity? Isn't it the ability to keep one's promise that makes a man of integrity? Yes! However, exactly *what* you are committing to is crucial for the outcome, whether you become a congruent and successful person of honor, or an unhappy prisoner of the convictions of the past, which no longer serve you.

The great confusion lies in the fact that we think that a single promise can extend for a lifetime. If this were true, the divorce rates would not be so alarmingly high, nearing fifty percent in the US alone. No one wants to break her vows, but it's difficult to pledge something ten or twenty years into the future.

Aleksey and I did not make a one-time commitment that stretched for years ahead. We did not agree to be together "till death do us part," either. Nor do we think such a promise is effective. When we decided to unite our paths, it was because we enjoyed each other's company, had a lot of fun, and shared a profound connection, affection, and mutual respect for each other. Each one of us felt that our love was the best thing that had ever happened to us, and it made sense to continue the exploration. The purpose of our marriage was to create a blissful life together and to experience more joy on a daily basis. We committed to the *quality—not the duration—*of our union. When happiness is your daily focus, those days weave easily into weeks, months, and years of magic.

Our commitment was not to each other, but to the purpose of our union. It is the vision of our relationship that continues to inspire us and pulls us through any challenges. Sincere appreciation for each other, deep caring, love, and the delicious feeling of kinship are our binding expressions. We vow to the sacredness of our love and to the greatness of each other's *spirit.* It is not the promise we made years ago that keeps us together, but the conscious moment-to-moment decision. We did not choose each other once…we continue making this choice every day.

Mikki Willis shared a great personal epiphany, where he understood the difference between commitment and devotion. He and Nadia arrived on an island in the Philippines to get married. But the moment Mikki took his sandals off and stepped on warm white sand, he got cold feet. He started panicking, recalling his first marriage and how it had not worked out the way he'd hoped, and worrying that the dynamics of his great relationship with Nadia might change and become worse. To find the way out of this emotional turmoil, he sat down in a deep prayer-meditation and asked for guidance and confidence. The answer came in an understanding of the difference between commitment and devotion.

When we commit to another person in a physical body, this bond is fragile and lives on the hope that no one messes up, because if one person breaks his or her promise, the seal is broken, and the validity of the whole deal dissipates. Devotion is a vow to God or the Source of Life *through* another person. Mikki understood that his relationship was to the *essence* of who Nadia is, which extended beyond her beautiful body. This means total transparency—there can be no secrets and nothing you can get away with, even if you wanted to. You can hide something from another *body*, or lie to some *body*, but not to a spiritual essence, which is omnipresent and eternal. This wisdom elevated their relationship above any of the superficial aspects, such as changes of their physical appearance or life circumstances. Devotion took Nadia and Mikki's commitment to a divine level, thereby making it unshakable.

Your future relationship with the *one* is a living entity, which is not static at all. It is not something you accomplish once and are done with it. Your romantic union will emerge, mold, and develop. You and your mate will continuously change and evolve. Learning to welcome these dynamics and embrace the transformations is invaluable.

Commitments only last when they resonate with your very nature and become an extension of who you are. Unconditional love is at the heart of all things. It is the lesson and the gift of a great personal relationship. When judgments are dropped and two hearts intertwine in sheer affection and devotion, the illusion of separation gives way to the bliss of oneness. Your powerful connection becomes a life-giving entity to new ideas, inspirations, and the physical manifestations of love—children. Then you are committing to the Source of Life itself, which is expressed through you and perpetuated through the union with your mate.

In reality, the only commitment you can ever make is to be the best version of yourself and to give your best to your mate every moment of every day. This is doable and rewarding in and of itself. Such a commitment does not require a certain behavior from your partner. Nor does it need recognition or acknowledgment from your mate, because you do it for you, out of sheer love and for the purpose of expressing who you are to the fullest. This solution works wonders for Aleksey and me and helps us feel free in a committed relationship. In the next chapter, I will share with you the vows we exchanged.

Our Wedding Ceremony

Our ceremony was intimate and informal. We did not invite guests or even notify anyone. It was our sacred moment; we shared it only with the reverend and two witnesses. We felt that the magic we were after was only up to the two of us. We did not want a showcased display for the precious feelings in our hearts, so we chose privacy.

In a park next to a blooming white oleander, we proclaimed the intent for our union and said to each other the words that were deeply meaningful to us.

Reverend: Aleksey and Sky have come here today, to make public their love for each other, and to declare their choice to

REMEMBER, IF THIS IS A MISTAKE, THEN ANY KIDS YOU HAVE WILL LIKELY REPEAT IT. DO YOU SOLEMNLY SWEAR THIS IS THE BEST YOU CAN DO?

162

live and partner and grow together. They decided to unite their paths to share joy, happiness, and to create a blissful and exhilarating life together.

Reverend: Aleksey, will you have this woman to be your wedded wife, your partner, and your companion for as long as you are both joyful together?

Aleksey: Yes.

Reverend: Sky, will you have this man to be your wedded husband, your partner, and your companion for as long as you are both joyful together?

Sky: Yes.

Reverend: Please join hands. Aleksey, repeat after me.

I choose you, Sky, to be my wife, my inspiration, my lover, my friend, and the mother of my children. I realize that my happiness is only up to me, and I will not hold you responsible to make me happy. I do not seek you to complete me for I am complete, but I seek to share love, affection, and joy of life with you. I look forward to dreaming with you and then living our dreams and growing together. I will do my best to remember who I am, and to see you for who you really are. Let our Love be unconditional, and let us appreciate each other regardless of the behavior offered in the moment!

Reverend: Sky, please repeat after me.

I choose you, Aleksey, to be my husband, my inspiration, my lover, my friend, and the father of my children. I realize that my happiness is only up to me, and I will not hold you responsible to make me happy. I do not seek you to complete me for I am complete, but I seek to share love, affection, and joy of life with you. I look forward to dreaming with you and then living our dreams and growing together. I will do my best to remember who I am, and to see you for who you really are. Let our Love be unconditional, and let us appreciate each other regardless of the behavior offered in the moment!

Reverend: We recognize with full awareness that only two people can administer the sacrament of marriage to each other, and only these two people can sanctify it. Neither my church nor any power vested in me by the state can grant me the authority to declare what only two hearts can declare, and what only two souls can make real.

Afterword

Dear Friend,

Congratulations on striving for excellence rather than settling for mediocrity. I am proud of you for taking these steps toward your personal fulfillment and creating a wonderful life. Your journey will be amazing and unique. I am very excited for you, because you have so much to look forward to, and you will be blown away by all the fun and bliss you are yet to discover!

You now have the keys you need to experience what you have always wanted and to call an extraordinary intimate relationship your reality. When you remain in the spirit of joyful anticipation and take pleasure in the moment, the Universe will deliver its presents in the most remarkable ways. Do you remember your birthday when you are about to open your presents? You know the gifts are there, but the thrill of surprise adds to the experience.

Don't worry about whether what you asked for will be delivered. Trust. The *Source* is benevolent and loving, and *The Law of Attraction* never fails. Be true to yourself, clearly know what you want, and firmly believe in your heart that your quests are answered.

The secret to an amazing relationship is very simple. It can be summed up in just two words: acceptance and appreciation. This means loving yourself and receiving your partner *wholly*. The art of love is in seeing the beauty in the "flaws" and focusing on sunshine above heavy clouds; it is in seeing new life in the face of death and knowing the immense power in the moment of weakness. The craft of love is in finding the reasons to appreciate and praise, versus finding the reasons to discourage or blame. It is in generosity and in an open heart. Love is in oneness; fear stems from the perception of separateness.

Don't wait for the special *one* to come along to start sharing your warmth. Practice being kind to yourself and to others now. Delight in the sheer giving, and remember to take care of yourself first. Your own fulfillment has to be a priority for you to be able to contribute. Expect nothing from others, but mine for the treasures in your own soul and offer them liberally. Welcome the support and care presented to you, because we need to allow our partners to express their hearts as well. Receive what comes your way, graciously and completely.

Whether or not you embrace the love of your life and dance together into the eternal tango is up to you entirely. When your heart is open, the lover will come—this is my promise to you.

In conclusion, I would like to offer you a practice section called "10 Days of Magic," which will help you open your heart and let true love into your life.

Practice
Section

10 Days
of Magic

*If all you did was just look for things to appreciate, you would live
a joyous, spectacular life. If there was nothing else that you ever
came to understand other than just look for things to appreciate,
it's the only tool you would ever need to predominantly hook you up
with who you really are.*
—Abraham-Hicks[12]

en Days of Magic is a process designed to propel you rapidly toward
meeting the love of your life. This daily practice will help you open
your heart to the flow of love, which will put you in a favorable
state to welcome the partner of your dreams.

For the next ten days, make *appreciation* your focal point. Look for
something to like in everything: your miraculously sophisticated body, your

---

12   Excerpted from the workshop in San Antonio, TX on 2002-01-26 For more information go to
www.abraham-hicks.com or call (830) 755-2299

home, your friends, your loved ones, your work, your neighbors, and much more. Everything and everyone has something for you to praise. I encourage you to become an inquisitive seeker of the positive.

The feeling of true love is akin to the feeling of deep appreciation and delight. By cultivating joy in your heart, you will become a magnet for even more things to savor and love. That in turn will pull the *one* into your proximity.

In order to accelerate your progress and assure immediate results, practice for ten consecutive days. Plan to dedicate fifteen minutes in the morning and in the evening to the assignment. It is best not to read ahead before you complete each individual practice in its entirety. You can practice by yourself or with a friend. Such a playmate can provide accountability, let you teasingly compete with each other, and make the process more exciting. For the sake of fun, there are a few games included throughout.

For the next ten days embrace your new daily routine:

In the morning:
- Stay in bed for a few extra minutes indulging in its coziness and comfort, savoring the relaxation.
- When you get up and look in the bathroom mirror, smile, and greet yourself with, "Good morning, Love!"
- Read the chapter for the corresponding day of magic. For example, if it's your first day then read the chapter titled *Day 1: Appreciate the Vastness of Creation,* and so on.
- Sit in a meditation-like state for five minutes, and focus on appreciating things discussed in the chapter. Fill your heart with warmth.

Throughout the day:
- Each time you notice something you like, make a mental note. Give it a bit extra acknowledgment than usual, and voice it to others

every time you can. Keep in mind the topic of your daily practice, and find more aspects of it to appreciate.

- If you are faced with an unpleasant circumstance, ask yourself, "What can be good about this?" Every time you catch yourself starting a mental rant about the badness of the situation, keep asking this question until your mind starts showing you the benefits.

In the evening:
- If today's chapter has a special assignment for the evening, complete it.
- Recall all good things that happened today. If you drove to work and every light turned green, or there was a very pleasant worker in a coffee shop, or your toast this morning came out especially crispy, remember all of that. Even if you had a headache and had to take pills, you can appreciate the fact that you have access to a painkiller and that it is easy nowadays to find relief.
- Share the best parts with others (your mate, family members, friends, or your action partner) in person or over the phone. Make sure to discuss only pleasing aspects of your day.
- Dedicate five minutes to meditating in the spirit of appreciating this beautiful day and all its gifts.

To make your practice more effective and enjoyable, I have recorded guided meditations for each day. To find out more and to get your copy, go to www.BestThingEver.com.

Day 1

Appreciate the Vastness of Creation

ost of us rarely stop to ponder the vastness of Creation. Trees, flowers, animals, birds—the variety is astonishing. Yet, it seems to be nothing in comparison to the immensity of space. According to the information gathered from NASA's Kepler space observatory, there could be as many as seventeen billion Earth-sized planets in our galaxy alone. To illustrate better the magnitude of this number, one billion hours ago, (which is about 114,000 years) we lived in the Stone Age. There are also other galaxies, with current estimates ranging from 100 to 300 billion. Our entire planet is a tiny dot compared to the Milky Way. The enormousness of the Universe hardly fits into our imagination.

All of these celestial objects move at super-high speeds and in perfect order. Our planet travels around the sun and through space at the speed of 67,000 miles per hour. Where does it get the energy to move so fast and so steadily? How do planets and suns know where to go? Why isn't this movement chaotic, if all of this is a result of a big explosion from billions of years ago? Extraordinary intelligence lies behind the miracle of life. It is the same grandiose blueprint implemented flawlessly on the macro and micro scale. All processes in the Universe are organized and interrelated.

The sun never fails to supply warmth and light. Our planet is nourished, and so is every living creature on it, including you. Nothing ever breaks, but follows a divine infinite plan. There is no such thing as an accident; instead there is a supreme fairness and profound purpose behind every manifestation.

Evening Assignment:

Tonight, spend some time looking at the starry skies. Ponder and appreciate the sky's beauty and endlessness. Notice how some stars and planets have different colors. In some cases the light you see took hundreds of years to reach your eyes, and we don't even know if these objects are still there. Every celestial body experiences its own evolution and undergoes an ongoing change. Appreciate the wisdom and splendor of the glorious movement of life, and feel your connection to it.

The *love of your life* may be looking at the sky and dreaming about you this very moment. Very soon you will be gazing at the stars side by side, engaging your souls in a timeless kiss. Fill your heart with warmth, and send your love to your mate, wherever she is.

If city lights or clouds obscure visibility, Google some images of space and contemplate its exquisiteness.

A game to play with your Action Partner:

Take turns recalling all things that you used to take for granted or simply not notice, but today felt appreciation for. Keep track of who names more. The winner will receive a five-minute backrub from the other partner.

It really does look like this beautiful oasis...in the backdrop of infinity, an enormous universe is behind it. It's a really moving experience to be able to see that with your eyes... Looking down at the Earth and you see the line that separates day into night slowly moving across the planet... And then watching the Earth come alive—you see the lights from the cities and the towns... Shooting stars going below us, or the dancing curtains of auroras—it's just very hard to describe the colors, the beauty, the motion...
—Ron Garan, Shuttle/ISS Astronaut

The events you see from space, like flying over thunderstorms, looking at them from the top was spectacular—like a fireworks show going on and you are looking at it from the very top.
—Shane Kimbrough, Shuttle/ISS Astronaut

Evening Assignment:
Find a space photograph of our planet, and gaze at it for a while. Imagine if you were looking at it from space. Then, settle into a meditative state. In your mind's eye, hug our Mother Earth, and affectionately connect your heart to hers. From your very core, express your gratitude and warmth. Bow to her in humbleness and offer service.

Day 3

Appreciate the Gift of Laughter

aughter and smiles are our first expressions of joy and happiness. Babies start laughing way before they say their first word. Mirth is the spice of life. When we sincerely laugh, our worries and stresses disappear; we forget about problems and get engulfed in the fun of the present moment. We receive an energy boost, our muscles relax, and our pains diminish.

Humor is one of our greatest beneficial gifts for overall well-being, including relationships. There is no better way to smooth the edges in communication than with a good joke. Wit and spontaneity are ideal antidotes to irritations or discontents. In a split second, they can transform seemingly serious disagreements into lightheartedness. Laughter breaks ice, helps to relinquish grudges, brings people together, and sparks connections.

It is no surprise that Dr. Patch Adams—the founder of the Gesundheit! Institute and a real person behind the famous movie *Patch Adams* starring Robin Williams—chose humor as an instrument to dissolve violence and bring health not only to our physical bodies, but to our homes, families, communities, and to humanity as a whole. Dr. Adams sees humor as a universal language of peace and compassion.

Since medieval times jesters were privileged within a noble or royal household. A fool was excused for his behavior and given a license to mock the tyrant. Jokers scorned inflated egos, stinginess, hypocrisy, and other unfavorable human traits. What people tried to hide, a clown exposed with cheerfulness and love.

Laughter adds zest and aliveness to our experiences. Its contagious nature is conducive to spreading joy and good mood. Share your smiles and gaiety with others. Today, forget that you are a serious adult with responsibilities and obligations, and be a source of fun and playfulness. Observe children and how easily they laugh. Embrace the same upbeat attitude, and allow yourself to be silly and even goofy. Skip a step, dance in the grocery aisle of a supermarket, and wink at the bank teller.

Buy a bouquet of flowers and give individual blooms to different people randomly, for no other reason but to share your delight. Read some jokes, and tell the funniest ones to your co-workers. Get soap bubbles, and blow them during a break at work. Better yet, bring a few of them to your workplace and conduct a contest for the biggest bubble; prepare a cute prize to give to the winner.

Evening Assignment:
Gather people who are fun, invite your action partner, too, and take turns telling hilarious true stories. Intend to set a laughter record for the night. Prepare some pop rocks candy and air balloons in advance, to make your party more exciting and set the atmosphere.

Day 4

Appreciate Modern-day Technology

Just a few decades ago, the Internet didn't exist; nor did e-mail, e-commerce, online trading, or social media. We've come so far in a very short period of time. When I was growing up, we didn't even have a phone. Did you? Could you imagine smartphones and Skype twenty years ago? Ponder the phenomenal technological advancements that have happened before your very eyes and continue to evolve at accelerating speeds. When you watch a movie that is only ten years old, it becomes apparent how much the technology has progressed.

So many household chores that used to consume hours now take minutes. Washers and dryers, mixers and food processors, blenders and dishwashers, vacuum cleaners, and refrigerators are modern conveniences that we often take for granted, but they make our lives so much easier. Aleksey and I travel a lot, and when we see people in other countries cooking on an open fire or spending hot and humid evenings outdoors because their houses are not equipped with an air conditioner, our appreciation grows for the luxuries that we're accustomed to.

are living expressions of divine wisdom, where various elements coexist and perform in the spirit of collaboration for the benefit of the entire organism—a human being. Wouldn't it be great if each person recognized his role in the health of the body of humanity? If we only realized that while there is an individual mission and unique life to be experienced by each one of us, our distinct purpose serves the well-being of the whole.

What a gift your body is! Your eyes allow you to see the beauty of this world—the face of your newborn baby, a mesmerizing piece of art, or dazzling cherry blossoms. Your ears enable you to hear music and the voice of your beloved, to enjoy birds singing and the sound of rain. Your refined sense of smell adds the realm of fragrance to your perception of the world. It is so complex that even the most advanced machines cannot recognize or reproduce scents. No computer can identify aromas in the surrounding air; no lab can replicate the exact nuances of the ocean breeze. Your voice gives you an ability to express your thoughts and ideas and serves as an instrument for your soul's expressions. You get to know and enjoy the deliciousness of food through your intricate palate. You discern textures and materials by touch and revel in affection through your tactile senses.

Your physical form is designed with remarkable brilliance. It is highly adaptable, with very strong protective mechanisms in place, capable of self-reconstruction and rehabilitation. Our highly effective immune system is constantly on guard protecting us from billions of bacteria and viruses we come in contact with daily. Isn't it amazing how fast our wounds heal and bruises disappear? You worry more when you scratch your car than when you scratch your skin, because you know that your skin will be restored with pretty much no effort on your end. Your car, on the other hand, cannot repair itself. Yet, your body is your main vehicle, and your hands, feet, skin, hair, etc. are your most prized possessions.

Look at your physical form in a mirror, with full acknowledgment of its genius. Appreciate every part of it. Embrace the uniqueness of its shape, size, and appearance. Your body is very responsive to your thoughts and attitudes, so be kind to it, and lovingly take care of it. Support its strength by providing enough fresh air, water, and quality nutrition. Take advantage of the variety of movements you can perform, of your dexterity and flexibility.

Today, especially focus on the way your body serves you. Thank every cell for being there for you and executing its function flawlessly. Appreciate your blood that flows everywhere, including the tiniest and most remote parts of your form, delivering nutrients and oxygen. Appreciate your fine-tuned nervous system that transmits signals promptly and regulates the overall performance. Offer love to your wonderful heart, which supports your physicality around the clock. Give thanks to your bones that keep the structure steady. Your body is an infinite source for appreciation. Provide it the attention it deserves at least for one day.

Evening assignment:

There are parts of your body that you like less than others, or of which you disapprove, or often neglect. It might be freckles, or extra fat tissue, or a bald spot. Study each one of them, and find three to five reasons why it is precious and is worthy of your appreciation. For instance, what can you love about your wrinkles?

1. They record your emotional history and reflect the path you've walked to become who you are today
2. They display warmth and charm and add unique character to your face
3. They represent maturity and wisdom
4. When fully accepted and embraced by you, they represent your self-confidence and poise
5. They reflect realistic unpretentious beauty—wabi-sabi

Day 6

Appreciate Your Accomplishments

A t times, acknowledging our own achievements is difficult, because our mind is too quick in discounting them. After I walked on fire, the same mind that was painting pictures of excruciating pain and terrible burns, feeding me possibilities of falling down and being scalded all over my body, said, "Oh, that was so easy! What was the fuss all about? Look, so many people did it alongside with you. You are nothing special; anyone can do it!"

We habitually focus on our shortcomings and forget our successes. Yet, it is our attainments that support our enthusiasm, propel us forward, and inspire future results. No matter how far you've come in life and for what destination you are headed, there are many accomplishments you should be proud of. Go as far back in time as you can, and remember every triumph you ever experienced. Whether it was a performance in a school musical or winning a sports game, learning a foreign language or writing a great essay, becoming a prom queen or kissing a girl you liked—each victory is worth a celebration. Were you accepted to a prestigious school, or did you volunteer

186

at an animal shelter? Did you nail a phenomenal sale for your company or compose an inspiring piece of music? Maybe you found the right words to soothe someone's emotional pain or told a joke that left your friends rolling in tears from laughter. Anything from a delicious cake that you made to a beautiful baby you brought into this world, from making a scientific discovery to putting your coffeeshop customers in a good mood deserves recognition.

Throughout the day, mentally pat yourself on the back for every success. If you made it to work on time, or completed an important task, or sorted out paperwork you were dreading for so long, or cleaned your home, or did grocery shopping, acknowledge everything. Become your own hero. This will show you that you actually do well far more than you fail, that you make progress and accomplish most of the things you want, and that there are certain areas you've truly mastered.

Evening assignment:
Get into a meditative state and remember the brightest, most successful moments of your life. Soak in each one of them, and recall in great detail how it felt. What was it like to exceed your own expectations? How did it feel to be a winner? Were you able to make a difference? Did you inspire others? Did you make your loved ones proud? Feel the triumph in your heart, and know that you can replicate and surpass your successes whenever you choose to.

A game to play with your action partner:
Have a party to celebrate your attainments. Take turns acknowledging each other's accomplishments. Sometimes, from the outside perspective, they are more apparent. Point out each other's special talents and skills. Appreciate your gifts and abilities.

Day 7

Appreciate
Your Home

A man travels the world over in search of
what he needs and returns home to find it.
—George Augustus Moore, *The Brook Kerith*

Having a roof over your head, along with all the modern conveniences, is a luxury most of us are used to. Over the years, our dwellings have developed to be state of the art. Today they incorporate so many innovative ideas, materials, and constructive solutions. We are much in control of the colors, textures, and the overall look and feel of our accommodations.

Walls and windows, floors and ceilings—many people put their labor and creativity into making these things. Hot and cold water, and gas and electricity are there to make your life easier and more enjoyable. Someone installed the pipes and power circuits, while others placed fire alarms and checked everything for safety. Your home's furniture, fixtures, accessories, décor, and appliances were designed, engineered, manufactured, marketed, distributed, and delivered to you. Your house is a collective product of so many people, and their service to you is worth acknowledging. Appreciate their effort in providing comfort for you.

Regardless of the weather outside, your home maintains the desired temperature and protects you from wind and precipitation. It offers you privacy and security. It serves as a foundation, where most of your days start and end. Yet, your house is much more than just a shelter. This is where you belong. The word "home" evokes warm and cozy feelings. It becomes an extension of your mother's womb—a protective, comfortable, and loving environment where well-being abounds. It is your personal space, which reflects your preferences and personality. Your unique style and vision came to life in the way you put it together. There are many special elements that you handpicked, as well as memorabilia that are dear to your heart. You get to relax and rest in the comfort of your private surroundings. It is a place where you allow yourself to be casual and authentic. This is where you connect with the people you love. A lot of your life happens here. Home is where you return and where you anchor.

Look around your home and soak in the appreciation for every little detail about your house. Bring up pleasant memories associated with some items. Feel gratitude for the amenities you get to enjoy daily.

Evening assignment:
Spend some time pondering and imagining what your home will be like when you share it with your life partner. How will you feel in your love nest? What ambiance will you create in your house? Will you need to update some furniture? What can be done to generate more distinctly the atmosphere of warmth and harmony in your house? Can you implement any of these ideas now?

Day 8

Appreciate Your Family

What can you do to promote world peace?
Go home and love your family.
—Mother Teresa

Whether you consider your relatives to be your family, or your closest friends, or both, is irrelevant. It is a tight-knit group of people with whom you've built a special bond. You connect through generations, and they are your fellow travelers in the journey of life. Similar roots, mutual trust, and sincere care are the linking threads of your kinship. You share with them celebrations and adventures; you call them for support and advice. Together you create a circle of compassion, warmth, and laughter.

Appreciate having these wonderful people in your life. Some of them paved your way into this physical experience, others crossed your path to teach you valuable lessons, and some simply came to keep you company. But without exception, each one of them carries a blessing and a special gift for you. Recognizing and accepting these offerings is an art, which I invite you to practice today.

You and your loved ones don't always agree, and there are differences in your characters and perceptions, but each one of your family members has some outstanding qualities to admire. You don't have to approve of their ways in order to respect their choices. You can shine your light of appreciation and affection and open your heart to them unconditionally.

Ponder the traits you especially value in each person. How do they enrich your life, and why are they important? Why do you care for them, and what can you learn from them? Do they spark your interest, provoke thoughts, present challenges, or help you grow? Maybe you simply enjoy being around them. Do you get to contribute to their well-being, and does that give you a sense of significance? Can you rely on their help and know that they will always have your back? They may be a source of comfort, affection, and tenderness for you. Are there times when they drive you crazy, but you realize that you love them anyway, and your heart melts?

Think kindly of every member of your family, and open up to receiving their contributions into your life completely. Voice your appreciation for them whenever possible. In the end, we are all pilgrims to the land of happiness, which is hidden behind the fears and barriers within our own capacity to love.

A game to play with your action partner:
First, take turns telling why you appreciate each other. Then, pick one family member that is the most challenging for you to love. Ask your action partner for help in looking for ways to appreciate this person. Write down at least five reasons why he or she is a gift in your life. Switch.

Day 9

Appreciate
Your Work

oing something meaningful is an integral part of our human experience. We consciously direct our efforts to achieve a result or fulfill a purpose, and we take pride in successful outcomes. Each one of us performs some sort of work, regardless of whether we are employed or a stay-at-home mom.

You invest your attention, creativity, talents, and energy into various activities. Inevitably you touch people's lives, whether through the products you make, services you render, or the demeanor in which you interact with others. Think about how many people benefit from what you do and how you influence them. Chances are that the input you made today will benefit someone for years to come. Draw satisfaction from the privilege to be of service and from your ability to make an impact and create a legacy.

No matter what you do, your every contribution is significant. While we hear on the news about astronauts launching into space or a president delivering a speech, there are people who prepare meals, do laundry, and wash floors for the astronauts and politicians, and thus contribute to their achievements. Whatever you do is of value to others.

Today, feel appreciation for your work, which helps you to improve life for yourself and others. Allow the sense of deep meaning behind your efforts. Nothing is too trivial, because it weaves into the infinite mesh of history of humanity and becomes part of the collective experience.

Let gratitude fill your being, when you notice that people are helping you. Acknowledge the salesperson in a small convenience store and the secretary in your office, the bus driver, the security guard at a bank, your waitress in a restaurant, and the bus boy, who cleans up. We are all one big family helping each other thrive. Your role is essential, because what you do serves these people back in some way. Appreciate yourself and appreciate them.

Your work stimulates you to constantly get better, improve your skills, grow, and learn. New ideas flow from inspirations; you explore your capabilities and expand your capacity. You meet different people, develop connections, and build relationships. You establish your reputation, and additional opportunities for advancement spring from your current position.

Your contributions are rewarded through monetary compensation, recognition, and acknowledgments. Your work provides for you and your family and helps to afford your lifestyle. Ponder and appreciate all the benefits you are receiving.

A game to play with your action partner:
Pretend to be young kids and play a bragging game called "My work is the best!" and take turns convincing your partner. Then, switch roles and tell another, "No, your work is the best!" and find ways to support your statement with new facts that were not mentioned in the first exercise. Keep track; the one who comes up with more valid points is the winner. The prize is a ten-minute backrub—a courtesy of the partner who lost.

Day 10

Appreciate Your Intuition

Your intuition is a priceless gift. It's like having a personal sorcerer at your side. When you follow its direction, things fall right on the mark with marvelous precision. Its subtle voice provides you with the wisdom of a higher perspective and paves your every step. It bestows knowledge right when you need it. It brings you creative ideas, warns you of danger, and saves you trouble. It doesn't take offense when you don't listen, and it persistently offers its benevolent support. Your inner guidance is always available and is accessible by calming your mental chatter.

When you are about to leave the house and forget to take something, your intuition sends you signals, which make you remember. Sometimes you don't even consciously register this hunch—you just grab what you need and move on with your day. However, when you acknowledge and appreciate the true source of your luck—your intuition—your ability to receive its messages improves.

Intuition is your gentle untiring guide and your very real earthly superpower. Remember as many instances as you can when you felt a nudge in your gut and acted on it. What were some of the best decisions you made by trusting your instincts? Appreciate these insights and the divine help you receive when this occurs.

Set the intent to be especially attuned today and to allow your intuition to take the lead. Let go of controls and hand the steering wheel to Infinite Intelligence. It's like giving in to the ecstasy of dance and allowing the melody to take you for a ride. Relax into knowing that you are in good hands and will be protected and cared for. Trust that the path will unfold before you, and pay attention to your sensations. Enjoy and appreciate this mystical knitting of spiritual and physical into the eternal lace through one common manifestation—you.

Evening assignment:
Get into a meditative state. Thank the invisible guides for offering their help and wisdom to you. Recall the times when you were able to decipher your intuition clearly, and fill your heart with appreciation and warmth. Ask for forgiveness for the times you ignored it, and ask for more clarity in the future.

A game to play with your action partner:
Share with each other your experiences of being especially aware and intuitive today. What kind of guidance did you receive? What ideas and inspirations came to you? How did your mindfulness affect your day?

Acknowledgments

This book would not be possible without my own best thing ever—my relationship with my husband. Aleksey, my heart overflows with appreciation of you—my beloved co-creator and life partner. You supply inspiration and continuous support, you give me assurance when I am in doubt, and encourage me when the going is hard. You help me believe in myself and share my victories. You make me laugh, you wipe my tears, you kiss me when I am at my lowest, and you help me spread my wings and catch a creative wave. Aleksey, you are a real blessing in my life and the greatest gift.

I would like to thank Rick Frishman for seeing a potential in me and for opening the door of publishing opportunity. David Hancock, for his open heart and warm personality, for seeing value in my message, and helping me to carry it out to the world. I commend your courage to follow your own dreams and for creating an environment where other authors' visions could come into being. My gratitude extends to the entire team of Morgan James Publishing, who have demonstrated efficiency, professionalism, and true passion for books.

I extend a warm thank-you to the amazing people who contributed their wisdom and stories to this project. I feel honored to get to know you and to learn from you. Mikki Willis and Nadia Salamanca, during our interview I felt your deep compassion and sincere desire to share the warmth of your hearts with others. Thank you for your generosity and care, and for invaluable lessons that came through the stories you shared. Amber Hartnell, your phenomenal ability to expose your soul, be vulnerable, and drop any reservations is truly remarkable. I admire your passion for life, and you are a role model for me in your feminine radiance. Mali Apple and Joe Dunn, you were always responsive and helpful. I appreciate your profound insights and bow to the depth of connection you developed. Dianne and Alan Collins, you were highly efficient and thorough in our interactions and a real pleasure to communicate with. You are inspiring masters of deliberate creation, and your purpose-driven attitude toward life is extraordinary. Peggy McColl, your fascinating journey into personal happiness and dazzling success is exciting and enlightening; much gratitude for your candidness and support. My dear friends and Magic Moments contributors, who amiably revealed their private occurrences—Tatiana and Anatoly, Kari and Colin—thank you for your willingness to inspire happiness in others and for being living examples of heavenly relationships.

To my gifted and attentive editor, Valerie Brooks. You have truly mastered your delicate art of perfecting the written word through your keen understanding of the audience and industry standards.

To Tim Ferriss for writing *The 4-Hour Work Week,* which gave me the courage to step beyond the habitual ways of a full-time job and pursue my passions. You helped me see new opportunities and discover my special gifts.

To the benevolent fairies of the Universe who playfully sprayed their silver dust on my writing journey, arranged synchronicities, and gracefully revealed every next step of the way.

Thank you!

Contact

If you'd like to contact me or to receive information on my workshops, events, and products, please visit www.BestThingEver.com where I will be sharing more insights and practical tools. I would love to hear from you!

About the Author

Sky Blossoms carries the heritage of her female ancestors, who were powerful healers. A medical degree combined with more than a decade of studying psychology, human behavior, traditional modalities, and metaphysical approaches lay the solid foundation for Sky's understanding of human relationships. Her knack for knowing exactly what stands in our way of true love is remarkable.

Sky's humble beginnings of growing up in Ukraine sparked her drive for extraordinary life experiences and prompted a relentless search for answers. Her personal journey through pain, disappointments, and failures taught her vital lessons and led to the discovery of unsurpassed bliss and fulfillment. Sky's own fairy tale relationship successes inspired her mission to empower others, which she leads with an open heart, compassion, and honesty.

Printed in the USA
CPSIA information can be obtained
at www.ICGtesting.com
JSHW022333140824
68134JS00019B/1454